MW00981595

SHELL'S GOLD

*by Lisa Bahlinger
and Michael R. Strickland*

SUMMIT
BOOKS

Illustrator: Sue Cornelison

Dedication

To Cliff, Sophia, and Linnea Bahlinger, my gold.
—L. B.

To Chelsea, Rebecca, Hannah, Cooper, and Paige Strickland.
—M. R. S.

For information, contact
Perfection Learning® Corporation
1000 North Second Avenue, P.O. Box 500
Logan, Iowa 51546-0500.
Phone: 800-831-4190 • Fax: 800-543-2745
www.perfectionlearning.com

Paperback ISBN 0-7891-5544-3
Cover Craft® ISBN 0-7569-0855-8
Printed in the U.S.A.

2 3 4 5 6 7 PP 10 09 08 07 06 05

Lisa Bahlinger is a writer and freelance children's book editor. She earned a B.A. in English from Louisiana State University and an M.F.A. in writing from Vermont College. She has received two fellowships to the Virginia Center for the Creative Arts. Lisa has written and published a number of poems and essays for adults and children, including several short essays in *African-American Writers: A Dictionary*, published by ABC-CLIO, 2000. She is a contributing editor to *The Other Side* magazine and is a member of the Society of Children's Books Writers and Illustrators. Lisa lives with her husband and daughters in Stone Mountain, Georgia.

Michael R. Strickland is a literacy educator, poet, anthologist, and historian who travels internationally speaking to children, teachers, and parents. Michael is a board member of the Maurice Robinson Fund, the Isaiah House Homeless Shelter in East Orange, New Jersey, and the Griffin-Bridges mentoring program at Seton Hall Preparatory School. He is a doctoral candidate in English Education at New York University and a graduate of Cornell University. Michael earned a master's degree from Seton Hall University. His other books include *A to Z of African American History*, *Poems That Sing to You*, *Haircuts at Sleepy Sam's*, and *African American Writers: A Dictionary*. A fellow of the Institute for Arts and Humanities Education, Michael leads workshops about using multicultural poetry across the curriculum and engaging readers and writers for balanced literacy.

CONTENTS

1

A PORTENT

My name is Michelle Minette Wilkins, and I've never kept a diary before. Overall, I think it is a dumb idea to write down your most secret thoughts where they can be found by your little brother and then broadcast to the world. But with everything that has happened and is happening, Grandma Blue thought keeping a journal might help me sort it all out. That's what she said, anyway, when she gave me this journal I am writing in now. This feels so weird, lying here talking to a book! Have I lost my mind?!

Shell put down the journal, picked up a legal pad, and started a letter to her best friend, Brocade. Shell and Brocade had been best friends since they were 12 and had been together almost all the time, in school and out. Shell sat up, scrunched up her pillows, and crossed her legs. She looked at the postcard from Wales she'd gotten from Brocade. It was really a photograph of Brocade standing on a farm somewhere. Just the idea was laughable. In the picture, she was wearing tall green rubber boots and was standing in a field, surrounded by sheep. If Shell looked closely, she could see that Brocade and the sheep were all standing in thick, sticky-looking mud. Brocade was smiling at the camera and shading her eyes with her hand. Her long, lovely hair was pulled back in a ponytail.

Dear Shell, You would love it here. The sheep are like big, woolly coffee tables, so calm we could lean on them if we wanted to. I'm eating lots of crumpets and scones and drinking tea with milk and sugar, like the Welsh family I'm visiting. Much love and see you soon! Just think, next year when I get back, we'll be seniors!!

Dear Brocade, Shell wrote. *I have to tell you what happened today. I wish I could just pick up the phone and call you. I can't believe you won't be home when I get back to Atlanta, that you will be off on this fabulous adventure without me! After all the vacations and trips we've gone on together—camping in the north Georgia mountains, shopping and going to the aquarium in Chattanooga, seeing* The Lion King *on*

Broadway in New York last year—how can you get to spend the entire school year in Europe without me?

Shell stopped to think. She had desperately wanted to spend her junior year abroad too, of course. But Shell remembered her dad saying, "Shell, honey, I know you want to go, and I want you to go. But it's very expensive, and we just don't have that kind of money. Besides, your mother and I don't think a whole year away is a good idea."

And her mom had said, "If you keep your grades up, maybe we can take you when you graduate from high school."

Brocade, are you still coming home for Christmas break? I hope so . . . What was England like? When will you get to Paris and start school? When does your mom leave? You'll probably be in school by the time you get this letter. It's hard to believe you are so far away. Anyway, about what happened today. I'm so upset . . .

Shell thought back on the day, but she hardly knew where to begin. She crumpled up the letter. What was the point in writing to Brocade about her problem when Brocade

8

wasn't going to be able to help her? Shell flopped down on the bed and sighed. A few minutes later she sat up and began to write in her journal again, slowly, letting the day unfold in words on the page.

Dear Journal,

I guess I should have known something was about to happen. My big clue was this—it had been a perfect day in a month of nearly perfect days. Today the sky was a delicious shade of blue, the same shade as jeans you've worn almost every day for an entire summer until they are bleached by the sun and faded from being washed so much. I was stretched out on an old pink chenille bedspread Grandma Blue gave me. She found it in the attic, in a box of Aunt Marissa's old stuff. Blue is Grandma Blue's maiden name. Her real name is Lily Blue Wilkins, but somehow Wilkins never took, so Ty and I have always just called her Grandma Blue. Anyway, she never throws anything away. Her little house is a wreck, but Ty and I love it. You wouldn't believe all the cool stuff I keep finding—some of Grandma's costume jewelry is fabulous! This bedspread I found was Aunt Marissa's, but Grandma Blue says I can have it. It is so retro that it's in again, with all these big cabbage roses embroidered on the edges.

Anyway, it couldn't have been a more beautiful day. Hot, but nothing like Atlanta, which is home. August in Chicago, and not a mosquito in sight. I'd spent the day laying out, and I guess I fell asleep in the sun. The next thing I knew, Ty was nudging me with his foot, asking me to wake up and go to the store with him for root beer. Now, it was more or less inconsiderate, in my opinion, for my parents to go and have Ty when I was 8. Now I'm 16 and he is 8 and a pest to contend with. Ty loves root beer, especially the kind that comes in the big brown glass bottles. So we went to the garage, got out our bikes, and took off.

I knew it would be useless to bother Grandma Blue when she was working. Grandma Blue grew up in New Orleans, and that's where she first saw portraits drawn—on Jackson Square. She told me she just knew that's what she wanted to do when she grew up. Can you imagine knowing your whole life what you wanted to do? She started to paint before she started kindergarten. Grandma can still remember sitting on the kitchen floor as a little girl, the cool tiles against her bare legs, with her hands in fingerpaint. She recalls the thick swirls of paint, the sharp, chalky smell of it, and the way the paper curled up at the corners if you used too much paint. "And, honey," she told me, "I always used too much!"

Mom had Grandma Blue make portraits of us when we were five years old, which was old enough to sit still for a little while, but before we began to lose our baby teeth. And part of the reason for our visit this summer was for me to sit for Gram so she could start a "coming of age" painting. That's what Mom calls it. Basically, it means sitting real still for long, boring periods of time and not getting to even peek at how it's coming along. Gram says painting for family is the worst because they'll never forgive you if it isn't perfect, but she says it smiling and with kind eyes.

Ty and I walked our bikes through the alley, then rode down the sidewalk and up to Ontario Street. Grandma Blue lives in a really small town about 45 minutes from downtown Chicago. It's cool to visit because we are absolutely free to wander around, and then when Gram isn't painting, she takes us to the city. The only bad part is that there are a lot of tank farms around, and on bad days, it smells like everybody cut the cheese at exactly the same time. That is a direct quote from Ty, of course.

Even though it is a small town, it still seemed

to take forever to go get root beer on a truly hot summer day when you'd rather be asleep in the sun and dreaming about driving your own car.

But as I said, Ty is only eight years old, and there is no reasoning with an eight-year-old. Try it sometime. It was quicker just to go ahead and take him than to try to talk him into drinking a nice, cold glass of, say, water instead.

"Shell, I am sooo bored!" Ty said once he caught his breath and we were riding along, side by side. Another thing about Ty—besides being incredibly stubborn, he's also quite easily bored. Getting no response from me, he went on. "I can't wait for school to start. Do you think I'm going to make the all-star soccer team this year?"

I looked over at him. Ty is not a big boy. He's skinny and dark-skinned and serious, and when he talks, he won't shut up.

"Maybe so, Ty," I said. "You run fast." I was still half-asleep. Ty is also a dreamer, and he'll go on and on if you let him. Anyway, by now we were at the store. I pulled out a crumpled five-dollar bill from my pocket. Mom and Dad gave me my spending money and Ty's too, for safekeeping. This root beer was coming from his money, of course. I was already doing him a favor just by taking him to the store.

We walked through the cramped grocery store part into the even smaller deli part of the store, and I took a one-liter glass bottle of root beer from the refrigerated section. It was incredibly cold. Once we paid for it and went out to unlock our bikes, we realized that we hadn't thought about how we'd get the root beer back to Gram's. Neither of us had a basket. So we took turns holding the bottle under one arm and riding one-handed. Ty was scared to do this, and I didn't blame him. Eight-year-olds are not the world's most coordinated people. But I was also annoyed by the whole problem. Ty is forever getting me into messes like this, then needing help to get out of them. I certainly don't remember being like that when I was his age.

So somehow we got home. It took about 30 minutes, I swear, the still-cold bottle of root beer clutched to Ty's chest by now. I yanked my bike up over the curb and called to Ty to hurry up. I wanted to get back to my blanket and dreams of my junior year—parties, driving, dating, straight As, maybe. Something to get my mind off the trip to Europe I was not taking with Brocade.

Just as Ty raised his bike's front wheel over the curb, he lost his grip on the wet bottle of root *beer. He dropped the bottle from his arms as though in slow motion, and it crashed to the street in a tremendous explosion of brown glass and root beer. We stood there in amazement, sweaty and thirsty, our root beer nothing but a big, wet stain on the street. The tempting smell was everywhere, making me want to scream. So I did. Right at Ty.*

"Tybee Marvin Wilkins! You idiot! You never do anything right! Look what you—" I couldn't help it. The words had slipped out, and I was sorry right away. Poor Ty. I wish I could have taken it back. Now I didn't know it at the time, but that was just the beginning of the bad things to come. In English class last year we studied foreshadowing and how Hamlet saw portents warning him of things to come. Well, that busted root beer bottle was a portent too, only I was too mad to know it.

2

PENNIES FROM HEAVEN

GRANDMA Blue was waiting for Shell and Ty inside. "Did you kids have a nice ride?" she asked. "I was looking for you." She went on without waiting for an answer. "Your folks called to talk with you. They said they'd call back in a while. Tybee, what happened to you? Looks like you lost your best friend."

Shell looked at Ty. He had two tear tracks running down his chocolate cheeks and straight into his mouth. She hadn't noticed his face was dusty until then. Shell sure thought he was a pain, but as he took Gram's hand and began to explain what happened, she thought he sure was cute too. He looked so little. Shell began to feel like a jerk since she was the one who had made him cry. But Ty is not a tattletale. When he told Grandma Blue what had happened, he didn't tell her about Shell

15

yelling at him.

"Mom and Dad called? What did they want?" Shell asked.

"They want to talk with you themselves," Grandma said. And she wouldn't look Shell in the eyes. Now, on top of the disappointment of losing the soda, Shell felt a new, sour feeling. What could my parents have told Grandma Blue that she wouldn't tell us? Shell thought. What would we need to hear directly from them?

Shell started to imagine the worst—maybe they were splitting up. Maybe her parents only seemed happy, and sending Shell and Ty to Grandma Blue's for the summer was just a way to get them out of the house so her parents could start dividing everything up.

Shell was setting the table when the phone rang. She nearly jumped out of her skin. It was her dad. He told her he had some bad news, but he didn't want her to worry because it could have been a lot worse.

"Honey, I was laid off from my job. You know how my company is headquartered in Europe? Well, somebody somewhere decided to close the North American operations. And that includes my office, of course."

Shell tried to take this in. "When did you find out?" she asked, trying to sound mature.

She sounded like she was about ten. When she got scared, she spoke in this little, high-pitched voice. She couldn't help it.

"The beginning of the summer, Shell. But—"

"What?!"

"But let me explain—"

Shell was so mad. "Are you saying you lost your job back in June?" she asked. "You knew all summer, and you didn't tell us?" Unbelievable, she thought.

"May. The end of May."

"Let me get this straight. You lost your job in May and kept it a secret from us all summer long? Why?"

"Because I thought I'd be able to find another one right away. And I didn't want you to worry," he said.

Shell couldn't believe her parents had known this all summer and had kept it from their kids. "Dad, I am not 8 years old anymore; I'm 16. You should have told me. I'm old enough to know stuff like this."

Shell's dad sighed. She was furious with him for lying to them. Isn't pretending like everything is fine for months a kind of lie? But there was more.

"Michelle, your mother and I have been talking. We—"

"No! Don't tell me! Not that too!" Shell shouted. By now she was practically in tears. She couldn't deal with this. He was going to tell her they were through with each other and wanted a divorce.

"What are you talking about?" he asked. He sounded confused and a little annoyed.

"The divorce! You're getting a divorce, right?"

"No, baby! Look, just relax a little, Shell. It's not about us; we are just fine. It's about school, your school. I wish we could talk this out face-to-face, but we have to hand in all the paperwork. I know you love your school, and you've done well there, really well. Your mother and I are so proud of you. But . . . you know it's a private school, and we are just not going to be able to pay that tuition and our mortgage on the house too. We looked at all our expenses, and your tuition is one big thing we can change. Your mom and I decided it is best for now for all of us if we stay in the same house. Then Ty won't have to change schools, and we'll stay closer to job opportunities. But Shell, it's gonna mean you changing schools."

"I'm sorry," Shell said, "I'm not following you."

"I'm sorry," her dad said. "I'm rambling.

There's just no good way to say it. But for the good of the family, you will have to go to a new school next year so we can save that tuition money. Now maybe if I get a new position in the next few months we could see about—"

"What?!" Shell said. She had never raised her voice at her father like this before. They were both surprised.

"Now before you say anything, just listen. Your mom has been working hard on this all summer, and she got you accepted at Rainbow High in the academic magnet program! Isn't that great?" he said.

Shell couldn't believe he said that! "Isn't that great?" He sounded like Mr. Rogers, like Mr. Rogers offering her cookies and milk for a snack, and wouldn't that be great?

"Rainbow?" she said. She couldn't help it. All she could do was repeat what he'd said. It was too unbelievable to be real.

"Shell, let's talk more about this soon. I know how this must feel to you, sweetheart, and I wish I could make it better. But I want to ask you just to think about it this weekend. You and Ty fly home this coming Tuesday, and we'll talk more about it all when you're home again."

What was there to think about? Shell wondered. It sounded to her like everything had been decided. At least, everything about her. "Dad, I just want to say this. You don't know how this feels," she said.

"I wish it didn't have to be this way," he said before they hung up.

Shell felt hot in her cheeks. So let me get this straight, she thought. We can stay in the same house so that Ty doesn't have to change schools? Only I have to? My dad loses his job, and I'm the only one in the family whose world falls apart?

That night Grandma Blue made pork roast, macaroni and cheese, and pennies from heaven for the kids. She liked to cook, but when she got into a painting, she sometimes forgot they needed supper. That's when Shell would pull out the phone book and order pizza. But tonight, Grandma Blue had a cloth on the table and her good china out and everything. It was pretty, but Shell felt like someone had died. She knew her grandma was just going to all this trouble because she felt sorry for Shell. Shell wished everything was normal again and they could go back to pizza in front of the TV.

"My mother used to say sugared carrots are good juju when you cut them like pennies and eat them with pork. I think they're supposed to bring you luck. Either that or money—I forget which. But she used to make them for me, and they always made me feel better. So eat up, honey. You could use some luck," Grandma Blue said, passing the food around to Shell.

"Money wouldn't hurt, either," Shell said. "Then I could stay at my school, and it wouldn't matter what Dad did." She didn't feel that hungry and pushed the food around on her plate. But she ate some carrots, just in case.

After dinner Shell went to her room—her room for the visit, that is, which used to be her Aunt Marissa's room. Since she was the only girl, Marissa got her own room while Shell's dad had to share with Uncle Martin.

Shell sat looking at the picture of Brocade with the European sheep. There are probably lots of good reasons to be glad I didn't go on that trip, she thought. Hoof and mouth disease, for one. She could go on. So she did, making a list until bedtime.

Still, it was hard for Shell to comfort herself. Before Brocade had left for her year in Europe, Shell figured she would spend the year reminding herself that soon they'd be seniors together and it wouldn't matter so much that she hadn't gone too. But now what? Now she missed out on Europe with Brocade, and it was not very likely that her mom and dad would take her after graduation. Plus, worse yet, she wouldn't even get to spend her senior year with her best friend. Has anyone else, thought Shell, ever had to start his or her life over as a junior? If there are such things as portents, then there ought to be such things as juju carrots, as well.

The last few days with Grandma Blue were pretty depressing. Just the thought of changing schools for her junior and senior years was like waiting for a dentist's appointment or for a grade from some big test you forgot to study for. Grandma Blue even set aside her painting for most of the rest of the visit to hang around with Shell and Ty as they moped around her house. Well, Shell moped around. Ty didn't mope because he didn't really seem to get it.

"What's the big deal, Shell? It's not like we have to move or something," Ty said.

"It's exactly like that for me! I have to move from my school and friends I've had for years to a new school! Where I don't know anybody! How would you like that?" Shell said.

Ty considered this. "You're right," he said. "But you will still be able to see your friends," he added.

They were up in the attic with Grandma Blue. It was Monday morning, before it got too hot. Shell thought, truly, the woman has never given anything away. Every school picture and art project of her dad's, Uncle Martin's, and Aunt Marissa's seemed to be up there. Most things were neatly boxed, wrapped, labeled, and stacked, but Shell was already sweaty and tired of digging through old stuff when she absentmindedly looked through an old box that was marked *William*, her father's name. Shell came across a small, faded blue and gray cardboard box. When she opened it, she saw the gleam of a silvery bar. A harmonica.

"Grandma, did my dad play the harmonica when he was a boy?" Shell asked.

"What's that?" Grandma Blue asked. Shell showed her the harmonica and the box it had come from.

Grandma Blue took the harmonica in her hand and stroked it. She said, "Oh, no. This wasn't your father's. This was your grandfather's. You know we named your dad after your grandpa, right? William. Only we called your dad Wilkie. I haven't seen this old harmonica for years, since before your grandfather passed away. I'd forgotten all about it."

"Grandpa used to play the harmonica?" Ty asked, reaching for it.

"I'll bet it was wonderful to listen to him," Shell said. "You must really miss it."

"Wonderful? Oh my, no! He was terrible. Just awful! He loved it, now, I know he did. And he was bound and determined to learn to play the thing. But I declare, he never did."

"May I have it, Grandma?" Ty asked, palming it. He breathed on it and then carefully wiped the harmonica clean on his dirty blue T-shirt.

"Well, I guess so. It's not doing anything for anybody up in this attic. I sure do miss that man," Grandma Blue said.

That night Shell sat down to write back to Brocade. She pulled out the card Brocade had sent and a new postcard Shell had bought at the Museum of Science and Industry in Chicago last week when she had visited it with Ty and Gram. The front of the postcard showed an old Model T, and Shell had carefully drawn herself in the driver's seat. She had colored the whole photo with some of Grandma Blue's Prismacolor art pencils so it looked soft and antique.

Hi, Brocade, Shell wrote on the other side. *Thanks for your card. Wales sounds cool. I really, really wish I were there with you. You won't believe what's going on. (No, I don't have a new boyfriend in Chicago.) My father*—Shell realized she was running out of room in the little two-inch space reserved for messages—*has lost his ever-loving mind. Shell.* There was no more room to write the word *love*, and anyway, Shell felt just the tiniest bit jealous of Brocade, who was probably on her way to Paris by now. Imagine, Shell thought to herself, real *café-au-lait* every morning, wearing a real French felt beret on your head too. Then she started to wonder what hairstyle went best with a beret—braids, twists, something short and sleek, all the while doodling a tiny Eiffel Tower in the margin of the card.

3

OUT OF
THE BLUE

SHELL sat staring at her trembling hands. She was sitting in a window seat on an airplane 30,000 feet above the ground. In the middle seat sat Ty, who was playing his Gameboy and snapping his gum. Shell tried not to move her head. She was trying not to do anything, actually, because she was concentrating very hard on not throwing up.

Shell hated everything about flying—the early morning rush to the airport, afraid you'd miss your flight; the stale air of airplanes; taking off with the whining engines powerful enough to throw you back against your seat; sitting cramped up against the wall of the plane, just a small room, really, crammed with all these other people. Some of the strangers coughed or sneezed, and Shell hated that too—what if they had some horrible disease they were exposing her to? Then there was the slow, spiraling descent to a runway, the sickening feeling in her stomach during the long minutes before the plane's wheels bounced on the ground. But especially, Shell hated the thought of being so high up in the air. What if the plane suddenly ran out of gas and dropped like a stone?

"Just don't look down. Read a magazine or eat something, but don't look out of those little windows," Grandma Blue had told her the night before. Reading and eating were the last things Shell felt like doing!

Then Grandma gave Shell a hug. "Pretend you are on a stage," she had said.

Ty was intrigued. "Like in a spelling bee?" he'd asked. He was busy trying to recover all of the dirty socks he'd lost over the last few weeks because he needed to pack them in his suitcase. As he spoke, he lay upside down on the bed, fishing a sock out from under the dust ruffle.

"No, honey, that's no fun," Grandma Blue had said with a frown. "Let's see—a stage at the Academy Awards, and everyone is clapping just for you—a standing ovation! All because you just won Best Actor. You are thinking about who you want to thank."

The airplane gave a little shudder, then another. Shell took a deep breath and closed her eyes. She imagined herself in a gleaming gold lamé gown that complemented her creamy brown skin and large, dark brown eyes. The plane jolted again, this time just as a car on a roller coaster going up a small hill jerks you when the chain catches it.

"Ladies and gentlemen," said the pilot over the intercom, "we are entering a patch of turbulence due to a nearby storm system. Please bear with us. For the time being, I'm going to ask you to stay in your seats. Flight attendants, please delay distributing our in-flight snack baskets until we are able to turn off the 'fasten seatbelts' sign. Thank you."

"Cool," said Ty as he rubbed his hands together. "Except I'm starved." He looked around for a flight attendant who might take pity on him.

"Ty, do me a favor and hush up," Shell said. *I'd like to thank my parents who are watching the award ceremony from home tonight—look, Mom!* Shell held up her Oscar in her mind. Would she cry or laugh if that ever really happened to her? Probably cry, she decided, just one tasteful tear though, and no runny nose.

Suddenly the plane began to vibrate and buck like a horse who'd never been ridden before. Shell's eyes flew open, and she looked out of the tiny oval window. The sky was still

28

clear and blue. There was no obvious reason for the plane to act like this. Shell grew dizzy. Don't look down! Shell told herself. Too late. She couldn't pull her eyes away from the window. The ground, now a smooth, brown quilt patched here and there with green squares or jagged circles of grayish blue, seemed a long way off. "I think I'm going to be sick," Shell whispered to Ty. "Get me off this thing."

"Hey, lady?" Ty turned to the surprised woman seated next to him on the aisle. She smiled at him. "My sister here is about to throw up," Ty said apologetically to the kind stranger.

She stopped smiling. "Oh, dear," she said and quickly gave him the air sickness bags tucked into the seatback in front of her, then showed him where the call button was. He began to push it.

4

HAVE A BALL

ABOUT half an hour later the turbulence was over. After she threw up, Shell felt better, but she was trying hard not to look anyone in the eyes. She couldn't believe she had needed help from Ty, the nice lady next to them, and two flight attendants. They had moved her to the aisle seat. They had all acted like it was no big deal, but . . . I bet stars never throw up on airplanes on their way to the Academy Awards, thought Shell.

The rest of the plane ride was a blur of time with nothing to think about but the annoying two-year-old girl climbing around in a seat across the aisle, from her mother's lap to the lap of the man next to her. It didn't seem to be the baby's father, judging by his surprised look and the way the mother kept blushing and apologizing. Shell dug through her backpack and found the new issue of *Honey* she'd bought at O'Hare before leaving Chicago. She pretended to read the magazine, hoping people might think Ty was the one who'd thrown up. Ty played a game on his atomic purple Gameboy. Shell thought how Ty was the type who really gets into a new game for a day or so, then gets frustrated. At home Ty liked to give his game to his friend Paul at school, because Paul was the best at video games in Ty's whole class. Paul would play the game to a higher level for Ty so Ty could win without having to go through each step himself. He's not a type-A personality like Dad, thought Shell. Ty's middle name should be "Chillin'" as in "Tybee I'm Chillin' Wilkins."

Katie and Wilkie, Shell and Ty's mom and dad, named her brother Tybee because on their first date they had gone to the beach in Tybee, Georgia. They had met in Savannah, Georgia. Shell's mom used to tell her that when Shell's dad picked her up for a blind date wearing highwater pants, she had stared at them thinking how she wouldn't go out with him again. But she'd ended up having a great time. He took her to the beach for a picnic and a long walk. He'd even brought a blanket to sit on and a delicious picnic he'd made himself. That was romantic, she'd say, and her dad would roll his eyes, but it was obvious he loved it. "All in all," Shell's mom said, "it was a good way to start a marriage—

have fun, be romantic, and ignore what other folks say."

"Of course, you have to start with someone who's got a good heart," said Shell's dad, "like Katie here."

"And a hard head like you, right, Wilkie?" said Shell's mom, and she would flutter her eyelashes at her sweetheart. Shell would have to leave the room, unable to stand them for another minute.

The toddler in the seat across from Shell and Ty began to stand on her mother's lap and rub her face on the seat back. She spied Shell and Ty across the aisle. "Hi!" she hollered, raising a chubby hand over her head like she knew the right answer. "Hi!"

"Hi," said Shell. "Hi, baby."

The baby's mom pulled her down by the legs and tried to distract her with the view out of the little window. "See the ground down there, Marie? Like a big ball!"

Marie took this in, then stood up again. She looked at Shell and pointed out of the window with some alarm. "Ball!" she announced solemnly.

Shell nodded. "Ball," she said back.

"Aavball!" said baby Marie.

Aavball? Aav ball? thought Shell. Have ball!

Sure, have a ball. Why not? Advice from a two-year-old—have a ball! Who knows? Maybe Marie is the two-year-old who will grow up to be the next Dear Abby or Dali Lama. Maybe, if she could talk, really talk, she could tell me what I could do to make everything normal again, thought Shell.

"Uh, Shell? Shell?" said Ty.

"What?" Shell answered.

"If you're not going to eat those honey mustard pretzels, can I have them?" He pointed to the tiny foil pack of pretzels the flight attendants had given her.

"Why not?" Shell said. "Sure. Have a ball."

5

HOME AGAIN

"**T**YBEE! Michelle!" their mom called. Shell spotted her mom and dad waving as she and Ty stepped out into Hartsfield International Airport in Atlanta. Shell noticed her mom was wearing a watercolory pink dress with white and yellow flowers. She looked beautiful. Pastel colors, which she preferred wearing, set off her skin so that she looked brown dusted with gold. Hair, nails, shoes, handbag—all perfect. As soon as she was close enough to touch, her mother reached out and said, "What's this?" She pulled at Shell's blouse with a finger and thumb. Shell felt hurt. She knew her mother might not like the new blouse, which Shell had purchased in Chicago with Gram Blue one day, but she didn't think it would be the first thing her mother would notice.

"Mom," Shell said.

"Michelle—I'm glad to see you. I really am," she relented. She reached out to pat Shell and smiled at her warmly. Then she looked at Shell's blouse again.

"What can Lily be thinking?" Shell's mom said. It hadn't seemed so shocking in Chicago, thought Shell. She had a '70s retro look going, with a batik handkerchief top, low-slung jeans, and clunky black platform sandals. Shell, who'd felt quite grown-up to be traveling without parents until she was sick on the plane, now felt tired and small. She noticed that Ty was still young enough to holler, drop his backpack the minute he saw his mom and dad, and run to them for a hug. Shell thought she'd look like a fool if she had run to her parents, but she wanted them to hug her, to make everything all right. The wish was so strong Shell had to blink back tears and pretend not to care about seeing them.

"Michelle, baby, it is so good to see you!" Shell's dad said as he reached for her, touched her cheek, and pulled her into a hug. His scratchy sport coat hurt her cheek, but it felt so good to be held, Shell hoped he wouldn't let go.

"Are you hungry?" their mom asked.

Ty piped up, "Yes. Starved. They don't give you food on the plane, at least not food like lunch food. Then when Shell got sick, even if I had wanted to eat, I couldn't have!"

"Shell! Are you okay, sweetie?" her dad said.

Shell didn't know whether to be angry with Ty for telling or to thank him.

She was glad to be back on the ground. As she rode with her parents and Ty on the trains to the terminal, she didn't say much, just let Ty fill up the air with his chatter about the trip and the summer away with Gram Blue. Shell wanted to stay happy to be home. She was so tired and still a little queasy from the flight. But she was starting to feel just a tiny bit of resentment and worry creep into her mind. Here was her dad— jobless! What had happened? Did he tell her the whole truth about how he'd lost his job? What would they do? What would they live on?

Once they arrived at the terminal, there was a wait in baggage claim for the luggage, and Shell's dad had to go on about how much Shell's bags weighed and how much shopping she must have done in Chicago. Shell played along, halfheartedly, saying, "Yeah, I got such a good deal on my shirt, I bought one for Mom too!" And even she had to laugh at the look in her mother's eyes.

As Shell dumped her bags into the trunk of her father's expensive-looking gold sedan, she thought, why doesn't he sell this car? She immediately began to feel guilty just for thinking it, as though she was being disloyal to her dad.

But the little voice in her head went on. Selling the car would give them enough money to pay her tuition for another year or more, maybe until graduation. And if they sold the car, they'd still have her mom's minivan until they could buy a second, less expensive car.

The good feeling of seeing them and being home had faded, replaced by a nagging feeling of resentment and worry.

As her father paid the parking attendant and drove onto the interstate, Shell watched her mother lower the car's visor and open the small lighted mirror. As Ty talked to their dad, Shell watched their mom take out a lipstick and carefully touch up her makeup. For some reason, this really annoyed Shell most of all, more than her mom's comments about Shell's blouse. Ignoring Ty, Shell leaned toward her mom and said, "Why aren't you upset? Why aren't we talking about what happened to Dad's job? How can you just sit there, put on lipstick, and act like everything is fine?"

The conversation stopped as though Shell had leaned forward and dropped a grenade into the front seat. "What are you saying, Shell?" her mother asked, wide-eyed.

"Dad's job! My school!" Shell's voice rose a little higher.

"Lower your voice, young lady. You are yelling at me! Now where did this come from?" her mother replied.

"This just doesn't make any sense, and I don't want to go to another school!" Shell said.

"Now, Michelle," her mother continued, swiveling around to look directly at her. "You've had a little time to think about this. Why are you acting like we just told you?"

Shell gazed back at her, speechless for a moment. "A little time? Mom—you have had all summer. We haven't. And why are you going to send me to some second-rate school? How is that going to suddenly pay our bills?"

"Michelle, Rainbow is not a second-rate school, for one thing—" her mother began.

"Why don't you sell this car?" Shell interrupted. "Then I could see that I'm not the only one giving up something!"

"Don't listen to her," Ty said. "I love this car! Keep it until I'm a teenager, okay?"

"Katie, let me handle this," Shell's dad broke in with a quiet voice. "Shell, there are a lot of things you just don't understand. Don't be mad at your mother. We are all doing the best we can. And anyway, as a matter of fact, this car is leased. My company leased it for me. We don't actually own it, so we can't sell it."

"Your company—that fired you—owns this car?"

"First of all, no, my company doesn't own it, either. They leased it for me from a dealer and have been paying the notes as a job perk, a reward for a particularly large project I worked on a few years back. Now that I won't be working for them anymore, I'll need to give it back. And second, I wasn't fired, Shell. The company likes my work, but this is one of those corporate HQ decisions to consolidate . . ."

"HQ?" Ty said.

"Headquarters," Shell said. "So, something else you never told me! Why didn't you tell me that about this car?"

"I'm sure we mentioned it. You were probably more interested in riding in the new car than you were in where it had come from," Shell's mom said brightly, patting her husband's hand on the steering wheel.

"Honestly! I feel like I hardly know the two of you!" Shell said.

"Shell?"

Shell looked up. Her father was looking at her in the rearview mirror. "I understand you are worried about this whole thing. The fact is, we don't have much money in savings. Your mother and I," he glanced at Mrs. Wilkins, who pursed her lips and flushed, "are learning we may not have managed our money very well. There were some bad investments. We don't need to go into all of that with you children. But you do need to know we don't have much of a nest egg to fall back on now while I'm looking for a job."

"Maybe Mom could get a job. Then I could stay where I am, graduate with my friends," Shell went on hopefully. "There must be other things you could do before you'd think about moving me."

"We have thought about it, Shell, all summer. I haven't had a chance to tell you, but I just started a new job in catering," Shell's mother said.

"Catering?" Shell said.

"Yes!" her mother responded with enthusiasm. "I used to watch my mother cook up big pots of this or that, and I like to cook. It shouldn't take me long at all to get the hang of it. But it will be part-time at first, so we still won't be able to afford to pay private tuition."

Shell thought of how her mother shopped and cooked. She'd go to the grocery store and buy just one bag of ready-to-eat salad, a presliced and buttered loaf of French bread, and frozen, warm-and-serve casseroles for supper.

She had grown up in the Midwest and still considered Jell-O a salad. She liked going to the store every few days and didn't seem to know how to make a lot of anything at once. Shell tried to imagine her mother leaning over a stove stirring a vat of bubbling something, but she could not. "So we are relying on Mom to pay the bills?" she said and thought, *eek!*

That night Shell emailed Brocade on her home computer in her bedroom.

Dear Brocade,

By now you should be in Paris! Email me right away and let me know that this address you gave me is correct. Where are you checking messages? In the hotel or at the college? What is the hotel like? Is it nice? I just got back home tonight from Chicago. My dad lost his job (he said his company is getting smaller or something and closed his whole office), and my parents are making me CHANGE SCHOOLS. I don't know how they could do this to me; they are being so selfish. I'll let you know more later, but it looks like I am going to have to start THIS FALL at Rainbow. I should be with you. We could have had such a great year together . . . Well, this is making me bummed, so I am going to say bye. Bye. Shell

6

HUMMUS

THE next morning Shell slept in. It felt good to wake up in her own bed. She showered and dressed, then went downstairs to the kitchen. She trailed her hand along the banister as she went down. Her house was everything Gram Blue's house wasn't: big, clean, full of people, and full of light. She thought about how her parents had considered selling their house, and she was secretly glad they'd decided not to. If they had, Shell realized she still might have had to change schools anyway.

The house was quiet. Tybee must have gone somewhere with Mom, Shell thought as she walked into the kitchen and peered out the bay window over the breakfast table to see if anyone was out front. She saw her mother beginning to unload groceries while Ty ran around in circles on the front lawn, whooping it up with their dog, a chow named Tiger. Tiger was clearly overjoyed Ty was back home and kept running from Ty to

Mrs. Wilkins and back again. Shell sat down at the table, yawning.

Mrs. Wilkins came in through the garage door, carrying several grocery bags. "Well, good morning! I was wondering if you were ever getting up!" she said. She put the bags on the table in front of Shell. "Help me put these away," her mom said before going out for the rest of the groceries.

"What are garbanzo beans, and why in the world did you buy so many of them?" Shell asked when her mother reappeared with more bags. Shell had lined up several cans of the beans on the table and was trying to find room for them in the pantry. "Did you and Dad suddenly decide to become vegetarians while we were away and forget to tell us that too?" Shell teased.

"Just leave those out, dear. That's for making hummus," Shell's mom said.

"Hummus?" Shell repeated and wrinkled her nose. "What's that? Sounds like that stuff Dad uses on his vegetable garden."

Shell's mom laughed. "You're right, I think that's what your dad feeds the plants, but I don't know for sure. This kind of hummus is a Middle Eastern dish. It makes a nice appetizer." She went out for the last bags.

Shell didn't know what to think about all the changes, big and small, since she'd been away. She felt irritable about it, about not knowing that her dad had lost his job and that her mother liked garbanzo beans. Shell didn't like the feeling that there was more to her parents than she knew.

Shell's mother came back to the kitchen, turned, and called to Ty through the garage, "Tybee, you make sure to put Tiger in the fence when you come in!" Then she continued talking to Shell as though there had been no interruption. "At least I hope it makes a good appetizer. I hope I bought enough! It's for a Friends of the Library fund-raising party my catering company was hired to put together. We don't actually know how many people will show up, but we are expecting about 50."

Shell took this in. "So when did you start this catering job?" she asked as she went to the sink to rinse the stale coffee from the coffeepot. She filled the pot with water to make a fresh pot, though Shell realized she actually felt wide-awake. This evidence of her mother's new job, which had been hidden from her, reminded Shell of the way her parents kept leaving her out of important decisions, as though she were a little child.

"Just a few weeks ago, so this is my first big event. It's the same day you start school. Anyway, like I told you yesterday, it's part-time for now, but they said I should be able to move to a full-time schedule sometime this fall if the business takes off. I was really lucky to find it."

Shell said, "I bet. Really lucky." She measured some coffee into the filter basket and pressed the ON button. "Is there anything else you want to tell me? If so, please get it over with now, okay?" she snapped.

"What do you mean by that?" her mother said quietly as she gathered up her garbanzo beans and the other groceries she had bought for the library luncheon.

"I mean, Dad lost his job, and you found one. Is there anything else you didn't tell us?"

"I don't understand why you are so angry. This is good news. I was really lucky to get it. I've been out of the working world for so long, and this is a fabulous opportunity for me." Shell didn't say anything, just stood watching the coffee drip into the pot and filling the room with its warm, comforting, homey smell. Shell's mom continued in a gentle voice. "Do you remember Mrs. Delaney? She's the mother of Melanie Delaney, in your grade at school."

"My OLD school," Shell couldn't resist

saying and felt her throat tighten with swallowed-back tears. Shell thought of Melanie, a blue-eyed blonde and student council-type, and of her mother, Lanie Delaney, who was usually chairperson of the decorations committee for school dances. "Yes, I know who she is," Shell said cautiously.

"Well, I happened to run into Lanie at the fabric store. She was buying whole bolts of fabric to make curtains for her old sorority house—she said she's the property chairperson this year. Anyway, she mentioned that she and a friend just started their own catering service. She said she was just the silent partner and that her friend would run the business. I mentioned that I would be wonderful at that and wasn't it a coincidence that I was looking for a new job! One thing led to another, and I was hired!" Shell's mom was looking through her very small collection of cookbooks as she spoke. "Funny," she murmured, "I don't see a single recipe for hummus!"

Shell thought of her mother telling country club Lanie Delaney that she needed a job. It must have been awful. Lanie Delaney lived in an exclusive, gated neighborhood in which all the houses shared a huge golf course as their backyard. Lanie Delaney had probably never had a job, needed a job, or wanted a job. Shell's face burned with embarrassment, and she wondered if Melanie knew her mom had hired Shell's mom to work for the new company.

"Mom, are you sure this is a good fit for you? Careerwise?" She thought of her mother's canned soup, of four little ceramic dishes of instant pudding chilling in the refrigerator for supper. Did her mother know how to make anything from scratch?

Shell's mom poured two cups of coffee and put one in front of Shell, along with the sugar and cream pitcher. She sat down across from Shell and sighed. "I think it will be fine. I know you like to laugh at my cooking, you and Ty . . ."

Shell began to protest, but her mother just held up her hand and waved her off. "But I do like to cook. I'm just glad I happened to run into Lanie. I have to admit she isn't my favorite person, but I think she's got a good heart, and the timing couldn't have been better."

Shell looked over at her mom, then slowly stirred sugar into her coffee. "Mom, is Dad okay? I mean, isn't he mad about all this? He didn't even do anything wrong to deserve this . . ."

Shell's mom shook her head. "No, of course he didn't. But life is like that. Bad things happen. We still have each other, Shell, and that's the most important thing. You know, we never meant to hurt you by not telling you right away about your father's job. Your dad just wanted to protect you and Ty so you could enjoy your summer. We thought he'd get something else right away."

"Has he had any interviews?" Shell asked.

"Yes, honey, but the only offer he's gotten so far was for much less money, and that was the first interview he went to. Since that first interview went so well, he turned that offer down because we were sure there'd be more promising offers to follow. I guess it just takes time."

Shell poured lots of cream into her coffee and drank it. She was feeling better, as long as she didn't think about school. "What's this friend of Mrs. Delaney's like? The one who runs the catering company?" Shell asked.

"Audrey Wilson? Oh, she's nice. She's from the Caribbean. Jamaica, I think. She's a little high-strung for a Jamaican. But that's understandable. It must be a little breathtaking to start your own business."

"Has she seen you cook, you know, as part of the interview?"

"Really, Shell, I'm perfectly capable. But no, I didn't have to pass a test or anything like that. I guess this library luncheon will be my test! I'd better find a recipe for hummus, and soon," she said and went to work on tidying the kitchen.

7

SNEAKING AROUND AND THE ENHANCE-A-BUST! MAKEOVER

JUST then the phone rang. "I'll get it!" Ty said, coming in from the garage. "Hello?" he said into the phone. "Oh, okay. Just a minute. It's for you," he said, handing the phone to Shell.

"Hello? Bitsy! I missed you!"

Bitsy was another friend of Shell's from school. Even though Bitsy was from a wealthy family, she was totally down-to-earth and constantly baffled her family by doing things like volunteering at the food bank and shopping at consignment stores for secondhand dresses. She called them "broken in" and said they were the best clothes to buy because they were cheaper and already soft.

Bitsy was horrified to hear of Shell's bad news about changing schools and why.

"That's just awful! What are we going to do?"

Bitsy asked. Then after a brief pause, she said, "I know just the thing. We need to go spy on this Rainbow High to see what it's like before your first day."

"School starts on Monday," Shell groaned.

"So we have no time to lose," said Bitsy. "We'll come up with a plan. First, we need to get the lay of the land. You know—go sneak around that neighborhood."

Shell was comforted by her friend's outrage on her behalf and also felt amused by Bitsy's desire to take action. "Okay, Bitsy. Come on over and pick me up whenever you're ready."

Shell's mom was glad to have Shell go out for a while with Bitsy, but she reminded Shell that she needed to do a little back-to-school shopping, not just running around. She took out her purse and gave Shell money for new jeans and underwear. "We won't be able to spend as much on clothes this year," she said regretfully.

At first Shell was angry. Jeans and underwear? That was hardly a back-to-school wardrobe. Then she felt ashamed and said quickly, "It's okay, I know." She wanted new clothes for school, but she wouldn't have asked her mother for money right now with the way things were.

Bitsy arrived half an hour later in her

ancient baby blue Volkswagen Beetle. Shell could hear the car far down the street. It made a sound—an uproar, really—that could be described as a death rattle, a car taking its last gasps. But the VW had been making those sounds for years, according to Bitsy's older brother Beau, who "gave" it to her for $200 when he got his first real job and bought a newer used car, a Honda.

Bitsy was short and pale. She wore her fine, light brown hair straight like a little girl's. She had serious brown eyes behind her peculiar, bookish glasses. If another girl wore glasses like that, thought Shell, she'd look lame. But Bitsy somehow made them look like the latest trend.

Bitsy showed up wearing one of Beau's worn-out oxford shirts untucked and frayed at the hem. It was light blue with sleeves rolled up to her elbows. She wore a plain white T-shirt underneath it and what looked like bowling shoes on her feet. Another trend she was about to start, Shell thought. Bitsy was from an old Southern family in which everyone had a nickname. They nicknamed themselves Buzz, Lulu, Beau, and Bitsy, and if they didn't nickname you, they either didn't like you or hadn't noticed you yet.

While Bitsy drove, she and Shell didn't talk

much. The car was just too loud, plus Bitsy, who was a good Episcopalian girl, needed to concentrate on praying that the car wouldn't stall when she had to shift into first or second gear, as it often did when it was running cold. But it didn't, so soon they arrived across town in the neighborhood of Rainbow High.

Rainbow had once been a grand old high school. It was one of the first built in Atlanta. Then, when white flight over desegregation was at its worst and thousands of white families left the city for the suburbs, there were years of abandonment and neglect. The school developed a bad reputation as a place where teachers were untrained and students were unmotivated to learn.

Now the neighborhood was enjoying a rise in popularity after years of neglect as families, black and white, moved back. The trends had reversed, and professionals who'd left the city moved closer in to be nearer to their jobs. The houses around Rainbow High, mostly Craftsman-style bungalows, began a swift and steady rise in value. Parents who'd worked steadily for years to improve Rainbow were suddenly listened to by the school board.

Shell and Bitsy cruised around the neighborhood, trying their best to look as

inconspicuous as possible in spite of the racket
and roar of the VW. Shell thought the houses
looked very cozy in a shabby sort of way. Though
they were mostly old homes in the same basic
style, people had added many creative touches
to make their homes unique. There were
brightly colored neighborhood pride banners
and porches painted in bold shades of deep
green, dark red, or eggplant. Tiny white lights
draped over fences, up latticework, and over
doorways were left up year-round, not just
for the holidays. Most amazing of all were
the trees—tall, thick-trunked oaks, slender
dogwoods, and cherry trees. Flowers spilled
from containers, hanging planters, and garden
beds. People clearly took pride in living there
and spent time outdoors working in their
gardens.

Shell's parents had bought a large, brand-
new house in an equally new subdivision years
ago when Shell's father had taken his job. Their
neighborhood had no old trees at all, as the
whole area had been cleared by the developer,
then leveled flat. Shell's house had only a few
young trees her parents had planted and the
usual few prickly shrubs around the base of the
house. All the houses were big and painted
white or cream with red or black shutters.

Imagine if someone tried to paint their house like that in my neighborhood, Shell thought as they slowly passed a fuschia house with cheerful sky blue shutters. They'd be in big trouble.

Bitsy pulled the car into the school parking lot and turned off the engine. "Ah, blessed peace," she said, slumped in her seat. "It feels like you were gone a year, girl. How was Chicago?"

Shell filled her in. Bitsy always made Shell feel warm, comfortable, and listened to. Shell couldn't believe she'd be going off into this unknown brick building alone next week without Bitsy or Brocade. Without knowing why, something her father said to her in the car on the way home from the airport came into Shell's mind. *"You won't be the only black girl,"* he'd said, as if he were offering her a comfort. But he didn't understand. It would be like starting over as a freshman, only she was a junior. She didn't know the kids or what they were like, and they didn't know her, either. Would they accept her here? Would they think she was stuck-up, coming from a private school? And what if she didn't like them?

Shell told Bitsy some of her fears. Bitsy didn't really get some of what Shell told her about race, but unlike some white girls, at least she trusted and believed what Shell said. Like about how some white girls at school had been cold and ugly to Shell because of her skin color. Shell remembered how hard the first year had been, before she'd found Brocade and Bitsy.

Shell and Bitsy walked up to the front of the school, which was two stories and brick with lots of windows. It was weird to be there on a late summer day with no one else around, and the only sounds were of the occasional passing cars, birds, and a couple of lawn mowers droning in the distance. Shell and Bitsy tried the doors, but they were locked.

"Do you want to try the side door? I bet someone is working in the office this week. We can tell them we just wanted to check things out," Bitsy offered.

Shell examined an old flyer or two stapled to a message board in front of the school. One showed the graduating class from last year with a message, *Congratulations to our seniors!* The flyer was neon green, and the picture that had been photocopied was black and white. Shell noticed that most of the seniors, 90 percent of them, were black. She felt strange and realized she had never been to a school that was primarily black. She didn't feel like talking to Bitsy about this, however, and longed for Brocade.

"I've seen enough for now. Let's go shopping," she said to Bitsy.

At the nearest mall, one Shell and Bitsy didn't usually go to, they ate chicken sandwiches and fries and drank lemonade. Shell noticed that more of the customers were black at this shopping center, and she wondered if Bitsy noticed too. Many of the smaller shops were Afrocentric. There were beauty shops offering extensions, braids, and straighteners; a dress shop with only traditional African dresses; a hat shop that seemed to cater to older black women; and lots of shoe stores full of precariously high heels in a rainbow of hues. Shell and Bitsy laughed a lot at stupid little things, as people do who are nervous about something that is coming next. As they browsed through the stores, Shell thought, Bitsy is only doing this for me, because she doesn't even like new stuff! But Bitsy mentioned she had school clothes to shop for too. They decided to go to the large department store that anchored the mall at one end.

"Let's go by the lingerie department," Shell suggested. "I need a new bra."

As they wandered through the racks of underwear, Bitsy stopped and whispered, "I know what we need!" She pulled Shell by the arm to a display of padded bras.

"Speak for yourself!" Shell said, laughing.

"No, really! It claims to change your life," Bitsy exclaimed, holding up a lacy, purple padded bra. She read from the cardboard card tucked over the hanger. *"Enhance-a-Bust! Guaranteed to increase your confidence along with your bust size, instantly, or your money back!* What have we got to lose?" Bitsy said. Shell scanned the area to make sure there were no witnesses, especially no guys, who might see which style bra they'd selected. Bitsy was oblivious, choosing the most flamboyant styles: the purple one and a racy red one with criss-cross straps.

Shell said, "Look, I'll try one on, but I'm not promising to get it, okay?" She quickly grabbed a black one, and they hurried to the fitting room. Shell was embarrassed to try on bras or bathing suits in stores to begin with, and the padded bra only made things more embarrassing than usual.

But when Shell tried it on under her short-sleeve shirt and modeled it for Bitsy, she decided she liked it after all. Maybe it was the silliness they felt or the panic about school. But Shell felt a little safer with a layer or two between her and the world.

"Wow. That will change your life," Bitsy said with a giggle.

"I don't know about my life, but it's bound to change something," Shell said. She bought a black one, and Bitsy bought the purple one. In an impulsive mood, Shell asked the saleslady, "Can we wear these home? You know, like little kids do with new tennis shoes?"

The saleswoman looked down her nose at them and said icily, "If you wish."

"Don't you hate that superior attitude salespeople come up with sometimes? What's up with that?" Shell said as they emerged from the store, carrying their bags with their old bras in them and wearing their new look.

"I don't know," Bitsy said absentmindedly. "I feel like Wonder Woman. How about you?"

"Yeah. You know, a padded bra isn't really underwear. It's more of a *device*. Or a *secret weapon*," Shell said.

"But is it a secret weapon of mass destruction?" Bitsy asked airily, looking down her nose at Shell as she imitated the saleswoman.

They couldn't seem to stop laughing. It felt great and awful, like the end of something, or the beginning.

8

RAINBOW

SUNDAY night Shell could not eat a thing for dinner. She could not talk to her parents, as she could think of nothing to say to them. It was their fault she was in this mess. If she could only manage to get a fever or to break a bone, she'd be able to get out of going the next day. But she was perfectly healthy, except for her nervous stomach.

Shell went up to her room as soon as her parents let her leave the table. She knew they'd watched her push her chicken and peas around on her plate, and they'd watched her as she left the room. Shell was certain they were talking about her now, but she didn't care. They had not protected her from this, and they couldn't help her now.

Earlier in the day, after church and lunch, Shell's mother had come to look for her.

"I just want you to know that when I visited the school, the staff was very friendly. If you need them to help you find your classes, I'm sure someone from the office would be happy to help. Or," she had said uncertainly, "if you'd like me to come in with you just for tomorrow, I could—"

Shell was shocked. "NO, I mean, no thanks, Mom. You know I'm too old for that. It might make you feel better, but it sure wouldn't help me." She imagined her mother walking her to class. That would be one way to be sure to get noticed, in the worst way possible. And Shell's goal was to blend in to the walls. She wasn't sure right now if she would even be able to make new friends. But she was no fool, and her mother would not be tagging along.

After dinner, Shell went online and checked her messages. She'd emailed a few times with Brocade, who had said very little about what her days were like. Brocade seemed to have decided that the best thing she could do for Shell was tell her all the reasons why Shell would find France lacking. Tonight, for instance, she emailed, *Shell, reason number 51, people bring their little dogs into the restaurants.*

Shell emailed back, *Thanks, Brocade. That's quite edifying. By the way, have the French discovered padded brassieres yet?*

Then Shell went through her closet for the

fifth time to decide once and for all what to wear on the first day—her new jeans, the Doc Martens. What shirt? Which purse? How did people at this school carry their books? What did they do about lunch?

She decided on a simple dark blue knit top with a Johnny collar. And the Enhance-a-Bust! bra, of course, for courage. She went downstairs to make some toast, which was all she could manage to eat. When she checked her email again, Brocade had responded, *Quelle Horror! I mean, are you kidding? Have the French heard about padded bras? They invented them! The school I am going to has classes in bra engineering!*

The next morning Shell felt like she was going back in time to junior high. Instead of riding to school with Bitsy and Brocade in the Beetle, she had to wait at a new bus stop to ride the school bus. Shell felt lonely and stupid, standing out on the corner of her street by herself.

Rainbow was out of her district. The magnet program pulled students from schools all around the area, so most of the kids had long bus rides to school. Because Rainbow was bringing kids from all over town, Shell was the only person waiting at her bus stop. For a while, as she waited, she wondered if she were standing in the wrong place. It would be an understandable mistake for her to make, missing the bus that way. Her parents would surely forgive her for making a mistake like that. The more Shell thought about it, the more convinced she was that she could, in fact, be in the wrong place. Or if it was the right corner, maybe she'd just missed the bus. Shell thought, if the bus doesn't show up in five more minutes, I'll just walk home.

Five slow minutes passed with only a few cars going by on their way to work. Shell picked up her bag and began to walk home, almost lightheaded with relief. Well, it's too bad, but it could have happened to anyone, Shell thought. Mom's at work, and Dad is out on an interview, so they can't take me. I'll just try again tomorrow.

Then she heard the bus before she saw it turn the corner and come toward her. It slowed down, then stopped alongside her. The driver opened the door with a lurch and a hiss of the gears.

"Hey," he said. "Are you waiting on the bus to Rainbow High?" The driver was a tall, heavy man with dark skin and a little light blue cap on.

"Yes," said Shell with a sinking feeling.

"Well, here we are, running just a little behind schedule. But nothing runs perfectly on the first day. We'll get on track in the next few days. Back when I was in the marines—well, Miss, you getting on, or not?" He eyed Shell skeptically, like she might not make the cut.

Shell slowly climbed up the giant steps to the bus, which had a number of empty seats, and chose a seat toward the back so the driver wouldn't be able to tell her any more about when he was in the marines.

It took much longer during rush hour to get to Rainbow than when Shell had gone with Bitsy, and it was quite depressing to Shell to ride there in the back of a big yellow bus. Shell sat alone and stared from the window at the unfamiliar route. When they finally arrived, the driver opened the door with a dramatic flourish of his arm and said, "Welcome back, everyone!" A couple people moaned, but mostly the kids seemed excited, hurriedly gathering things together and getting off the bus. Shell felt as reluctant to get off the bus as she had been to get onto it. *I wonder why they call it Rainbow,* she thought to herself as she opened one of the front doors that had been locked when she'd spied on the school with Bitsy. *And if this is the rainbow, where's the pot of gold?*

Despite her nervousness, the day flew by for Shell. She had a hard time finding two of her morning classes, but she managed to find them before the late bell rang. She couldn't find the girls' bathroom at all until after lunch, and by then she was desperate. Shell didn't want to ask anyone to show her because she didn't want to draw attention to herself. Lunchtime was tough to get through. Shell took her tray and walked to the end of a table to eat alone. She swallowed hard, feeling sorry for herself and missing the time to talk and laugh with her friends. Shell pushed the thoughts of her old school from her mind. It won't help me to think about that, she thought. As she ate, Shell recognized some of the incoming freshmen from the halls by the confused looks on their faces. So she wasn't the only person eating alone. She wondered if she looked that way too—lost and a little lonely.

Shell found the school's layout fairly easy to understand. She was glad it was an old building with a simple design: staircases on both sides and lots of windows. Shell thought of some of the new buildings she'd seen—long, windowless one-story buildings that seemed to snake around into hall after hall. At least she already knew where all of her classes were. The harder part for Shell was that, except for the freshmen, people all seemed to know one another. Between classes, Shell found herself navigating a sea of bodies with shouts, waving arms, hugs, screeches, and slamming lockers all competing for attention. She was struck by a sudden thought: most of the other students were black too, and the few light-skinned people stood out. She realized that she *was* blending in because she was in the majority. Shell had always been one of the few dark-skinned children in every class as she grew up. She had learned how to walk, talk, and relate to white people so that they accepted her. She realized that here she wasn't sure how to *be*.

Shell carried all of her books until before her last class when she finally happened upon her locker. It was outside the performing arts room, which was located in a small building by itself beside the school. Drama was Shell's last class of the day, a class she'd been looking forward to. She peered inside the open door of the class as she dumped her books into her locker. It wasn't like a regular classroom. There were no desks, just folding chairs around the edges of the room, which was painted black and had a square wooden stage in the middle, also painted black.

Shell was excited. At her old school, there was no real stage for performances. People who took drama had to make do with a corner of the cafeteria as their classroom space. Shell didn't know which she had hated more: the smells of hot dogs and cabbage that had drifted out of the kitchen as her acting class had practiced plays or the clash of falling pans that occasionally broke through quiet moments of class.

The acting class at Rainbow had only 15 students. Shell thought it would be wonderful to have all that space to themselves. There was plenty of room for everyone to stretch out for the warm-up exercises. Shell was startled when the teacher walked in.

Mrs. Evelyn Wheat was a very large woman. Her very presence was dramatic. She had extremely pale skin and long brown hair, pulled back in an untidy pile on her head. When she entered the room, the other students, who had been talking and laughing, fell silent. Mrs. Wheat spotted Shell and walked straight to her, wearing a frown.

"You are a new student. Is that right?"

Shell nodded.

"Did you just move to Atlanta, or are you a transfer student?" Mrs. Wheat asked.

"I transferred from Wainscott Academy." Shell spoke softly but she was aware the other students were listening.

"Welcome to Rainbow. I'm Evelyn Wheat. I think there may have been a mistake in your class schedule. This is my advanced placement acting class, and you may only register for this course by invitation," Mrs. Wheat said firmly.

Shell flushed. "By whose invitation?" she asked.

"Mine," said Mrs. Wheat. "Please come with me. The rest of you, warm up."

Shell rose and followed Mrs. Wheat to her office, which was off the hall where the lockers were. Mrs. Wheat sat at her desk and began to read over some papers. Shell felt panic rise in her. This woman couldn't make her drop this class. Shell wanted to stay in. It was the first place in the school she'd felt at home.

"Mrs. Wheat?" Shell said.

Evelyn Wheat looked up from the papers in front of her. "Yes?"

"Mrs. Wheat, I have taken acting for two years at Wainscott. I want to take this class, and I hope you'll let me stay." Shell was trying to remain calm, but she kept squeezing her hands together as she spoke. Her hands were like ice. She couldn't seem to warm them.

"Well, first off, no one calls me Mrs. Wheat. It's a ridiculous name, belongs to my ex-husband, Leon, and it suits him. Call me Evelyn.

Second, I see you really would like to stay. But I know nothing about you or whether you have any talent for this subject. Some people want to take acting because they think it will be an easy A. You aren't thinking that, are you?" she asked, looking at Shell through narrowed eyes, as though trying to read her. Shell shook her head.

"Well," Evelyn said again, "the only fair thing is for you to audition for me. I'll let you stay if you pass the audition; you transfer to a different elective if you don't pass. Here," she said, tossing a small blue booklet to Shell across the desk. "Memorize a three- to five-minute scene from *A Raisin in the Sun* for me by next Monday. You can choose to play any of the female characters. I'll read the other parts out loud for you during the audition. Oh, and you will audition in front of the class."

"In class," Shell repeated weakly.

"Yes," said Evelyn irritably. "It is an acting class. We'll be doing lots of that this year, so if you aren't comfortable by yourself on stage—"

"Oh, no, I'll be fine," Shell said. She wondered if Evelyn was just trying to discourage her. "Thank you."

9

HUMMUS AND HUMMUS

SHELL climbed down off the bus with relief. She was exhausted. To think she had to interview on stage alone to stay in the acting class! As Brocade would say, *"Quelle horror!"* Had the other people all interviewed in front of a class as well, or had they been able to interview alone for Evelyn?

When Shell got home, the door was unlocked. "Hello?" She called. Tiger came racing up to her with a happy yip and lots of tail wagging. "Anybody home?" she called, dropping her bag and a few notebooks at the foot of the stairs.

"Ty's at soccer practice, and I'm in here," her mother called from the kitchen. She sounded stuffed up.

Shell walked into the kitchen, then stopped. Her mother was sitting at the table with her head in her arms. "Mom, what's wrong?" Shell asked, worried.

Shell's mom lifted her face and managed a weak smile. She was wearing heels and a pale pink dress, but her mascara was smeared around her eyes.

"Well, hi there, honey. How was your first day?" her mom said brightly as she tried to wipe away the tears and the mascara with the backs of her hands. This only made the mess worse.

"MOM! I asked you what's wrong!" Shell said, sinking into a chair next to her mother and touching her on the cheek.

"Remember how I told you today was the library luncheon, and how it would be my big test to see if I could do this?" her mother asked, taking a few deep breaths.

"Yes, yes? And you were making hummus," Shell said.

"Oh, hummus! I never want to hear that word again!" Shell's mother wailed, then broke down into a fresh outburst of tears.

Shell's father came in from the backyard. He was wearing old khakis and an ancient Braves T-shirt. He had left his dirty boots and garden gloves on the patio. "Hey, baby, how'd it go?" he asked.

"It was okay," Shell said. "What happened to Mom? Something about the luncheon and hummus," Shell said as she patted her mother's shoulder.

Her father grinned. "I'm terrible, I know. I got no business laughing. But I can't help it," and he stood there trying to wipe the grin from his face and failing.

"Wilkie! Shame on you," Shell's mother said, standing up to shake a finger at Shell's dad.

"Will someone please tell me what happened?" Shell pleaded.

"I tried, I really did," Shell's mom explained. "I just couldn't find a hummus recipe, and I didn't want to ask Audrey at work for it because I wanted her to think I'd made it before. That was my first mistake. So I knew you made it with garbanzo beans and that hummus is a kind of a dip, but I didn't know what else went in it. And then Audrey told me she was making an eggplant dip to go with it and to be sure to use good sesame paste in the hummus. So I knew I needed to use sesame seeds somehow, ground up."

"So," Shell's father interrupted, grinning again, "your mom didn't know you could buy them already ground up, and she ground her own in the blender. They weren't exactly smooth, and she didn't know how much to use. Well, your mom made gallons of this stuff, and she didn't know she was supposed to put all of it in the blender together. So hers had whole beans in this squishy sesame stuff . . ." Shell's mother glared at him, and he put an arm around her. "Plus," he continued, "only 20 people showed up, not 50."

"Eighteen," Shell's mom said. "Only 18 people showed up, and none of them liked hummus."

"Or if they did, they just didn't recognize it!" Shell's dad said, laughing again.

Shell's mom smiled.

"At least Audrey was gracious about it. She just said, 'That's okay, Katie. Bad luck. But we're gonna have to get you some cookbooks.' That was the good part. The bad part was, she gave me all the leftover hummus to bring home!" Shell's mom opened the refrigerator door, and there were three huge plastic bowls filled with the stuff taking up most of the shelf space.

"Do we have to eat that for supper?" Shell asked.

"I won't put us through it," Shell's mom said with a laugh. "But, Wilkie, do you think you'll be able to use this hummus in your garden?"

"I might be able to use it in the compost bin," he said doubtfully.

"It'll get better, Mom," Shell said, hugging

her mother.

"So, Shell. Tell us about your day." Shell's mother poured all of them a glass of cold, sweet tea, and Shell told them grudgingly about the drama interview, and the bus being late, and that she wanted to take her own lunch from now on.

"But not hummus," she added.

10

TALKING GHETTO

SHELL spent the rest of the week getting used to her new routine. The second day she wore jeans and a white peasant blouse, and a senior named Maya stared at her as she got on the bus. Maya turned to her seatmate and said, "Kayrin! Look who think she all that? Miss Relaxer. She all dolled up for school lookin' like her mama dressed her!"

Shell's face burned as she walked past them, pretending not to hear. A few seats behind Maya, Shell recognized a boy from her drama class. Shell sat down in an empty seat right behind him. He'd evidently overheard what had happened with Maya, because once the bus was going again, he turned back and said quietly, "Don't pay any attention to them. They're just jealous."

Shell gave him a small smile, but she didn't say anything. She didn't want to talk about it.

"I'm Malcolm," he said.

"I recognized you from acting class. I'm Shell," she said with a nod.

"Shell, as in *sea shell*?" He asked, raising one eyebrow at her. Shell noticed that he was cute.

"Shell, as in *Michelle*," Shell said.

Shell wondered later why her parents didn't ask her how it felt for her to be at a school where most of the students were black, where she was not in the minority racially. She didn't know if they were even thinking about what this change was like for her. Maybe they assumed it was a change for the better. Shell brooded, wondering why they didn't ask her more questions about school. But when they did, she was angry that they wouldn't leave her alone. Why should she have to tell them about how hard it was? Shell thought her father should just know what she was going through and try to do more to fix this. Why should she have to make all these changes? What about him? Wasn't this all his fault?

After the Maya incident, Shell was very careful about what she wore to school. She deliberately picked clothing like what the other girls were wearing. The girls at Wainscott had been into a shabby, preppy look. But the kids at Rainbow dressed way down. When she saw Maya wearing a ripped pair of bell bottoms, a tank top, chain belt, black nail polish, and biker boots, Shell wanted to laugh because it looked like a costume designer had dressed *her*.

And what was the big deal about her hair? Shell had been relaxing it since she was in high school, and she liked the soft, straight way she wore it now, long enough to almost brush against her shoulders. But Maya's shrewd comment had hurt. Shell caught herself staring in mirrors critically. Maybe she needed a new look.

Brocade, what do you think about braids? I'm thinking about getting some. Shell. P.S. What's up in Paris?

Shell, you aren't the braids type. What is that school doing to you? What's next, dreadlocks? Reason number #245 you wouldn't like Paris—people eat snails and goose livers. Brocade.

What does she know? thought Shell irritably. What does that mean, "You aren't the braids type"? Who does she think she is, my mother? Does she have to worry about fitting in at a new school? No, she gets to be the happy-go-lucky American who gets to leave in a year. Brocade doesn't even have to try to fit in, Shell thought.

She decided to call and make an

appointment for Saturday at one of the hairstyling salons at the mall she'd gone to with Bitsy. Then she picked up the phone to call Bitsy to see if she wanted to go along. Maybe Bitsy would get braids too, Shell thought. That would be one surefire way to drive her mother crazy.

Shell and Malcolm started sitting by each other on the bus. Shell told Malcolm about how she'd transferred to Rainbow from a private school, but she didn't go into why her parents had made her transfer, and Malcolm drew his own conclusions.

Friday afternoon as they rode home from school, he said earnestly, "See, those girls at Wainscott must have nicknamed you *Shell*. That sounds white—*Shell* for *Michelle*. If you'd been going to Rainbow since you were a freshman, you'd be going around as M'shelle now. See the difference?"

"Yeah, I see it. But there's nothing wrong with Shell. If I didn't like it, I'd go by Michelle, now, wouldn't I?" Shell said defensively. She thought of her friend Bitsy, who had indeed helped her come up with a nickname, seeing as how her family was so good at that.

Malcolm put his hands on her shoulders. "Relaaaaaaaaaaaax. M'shelle is fine. Shell is fine. I didn't mean anything by it. Hey, look—call me

Malcolm, call me Mal, just call me, okay?"

Shell blushed, and Malcolm let his hands drop. "I didn't upset you, did I? I mean, I like to kid around and all, but I really do like you, Shell."

"Wow, thanks, Mal. I like you too," Shell said, trying to sound like a star-struck groupie. She batted her eyelashes at him the way she'd seen her mom do to her dad.

"You just need some help, that's all," Malcolm continued, straightening his jacket. "And I'm just the man who can help."

"What? What kind of help can you give me?" Shell asked, amused.

"Watch out now! What do you mean, 'What kind of help can you give me?' " he mimicked. "You need to learn how to talk ghetto, and I'll be your foreign language instructor."

"Oh! That's my problem!" Shell said. "I need to learn to talk ghetto. Then my problems will be solved."

"I didn't say that," Malcolm objected mildly. "But it'll help. You not at Wainscott anymore, honey, you at Rainbow now," he said. The bus pulled up to Shell's bus stop.

Shell shouldered her purse and made her way off the bus. Malcolm followed.

"Mal! You aren't supposed to get off here!

What are you up to?" Shell said as she turned and saw him tagging along.

"I live a few blocks over. It's not too far from here. I'll walk home when the lesson's over."

"What lesson?" Shell asked, amazed.

"Girl, you going to fail this class you don' pay me no mind. This be Ghetto Talk 101." Malcolm pulled his baggy jeans down a little lower and turned his baseball cap sideways, then slouched back and strutted, his thumb and little finger extended. "All right now, M'shelle, here be the verbs. I be goin', you be goin', we be goin'."

"I be going," Shell said, rolling her eyes, one hand on her hip.

"Oh, girl, I like that hip thang you got goin', but it's *goin'*, not *go-ing*," Malcolm said. "Or even go-ang, as in 'I be *goang*.' Check it out," he said.

"Yo, check this out. I'm gone, Mal." Shell walked by him and toward her house.

"Hey, that was pretty good, Shell, for a first lesson. Yo, wait up!"

Shell sighed and turned.

Malcolm pulled his jeans back up and looked at Shell, then away. "Is it okay if I call you sometime?"

He caught Shell by surprise. He was usually so busy being funny that she didn't know what to make of him when he turned serious.

"Straight up?" she asked.

"Straight up," he said. "I'd really like to call you."

"Okay," she said, and he wrote her number on his hand in ink.

Ty was waiting for her inside. "Who was that guy you were talking to?" he demanded, rubbing his harmonica on his jeans.

"None of your business," Shell snapped.

Ty made a face, then blew into the harmonica. It sounded like a wheezing accordion. "Shell's got a boyfriend," Ty sang in a sing-songy voice. "Shell's got a boyfriend." He blew into the harmonica again with the same result.

"Ty," Shell said, "Grandpa William would be proud. I bet you play just like he did."

"Really?" Ty asked, flattered but unsure.

"Yep, really. BADLY," Shell said, then ran up the stairs to her room with Ty in hot pursuit.

11

SHADOW

"**HELLO,** we're home," Shell called happily as she and Bitsy walked in the front door. They walked through the hall and dropped their purses and keys on the kitchen table. "Anybody ready to see the new me?" Shell paused, but there was no answer. "Anybody home?" she called. "Geez, why are they never around when I want them to be? Do you know Ty has been following me around with that stupid harmonica for weeks, but now that I want them to be here . . ." she trailed off, disgusted.

"Just be glad you don't have an older brother," Bitsy commented. "They truly make your life miserable."

Shell walked to the downstairs bathroom to study herself in the mirror while Bitsy helped herself to a Coke from the refrigerator. Shell looked at herself with surprise that a hairstyle could make such a difference.

"So . . . wow. You look great. Like Charlene

Hunter-Goff on the news. Very political, you know?" Bitsy said as she leaned in the doorway admiring her friend. The hairstylist had taken all morning to weave extensions into her hair, and now her head felt—tight and heavy with the weight of the new braids.

The new style suited Shell. It drew attention to her eyes and to her full, rounded lips. Shell touched her head tentatively, then, with more confidence, ran her fingers through the braids.

"Hey, Shell. You have got to feed me some lunch. What's to eat around here?" Bitsy whined. She was always hungry. She looked in the refrigerator again and came out with an armload of sandwich fixings. "I wonder what your folks will say about your hair. Did they like the idea?" she asked as she looked around for some bread.

"I didn't exactly tell them what I was going to do," Shell said.

"You what? You didn't tell them! Are they ever going to be surprised," Bitsy said dryly.

"Oh, please," Shell said. "It's not like I need their permission or anything. My dad will probably nominate me for Miss Black America, and my mom will say I look like a derelict."

Then Shell thought of Brocade—what would Brocade think? Shell could imagine Brocade's reaction. She pictured Brocade lounging at a café table with an expensive bottle of mineral water in front of her, shaking her head and saying, *"What did you do this time, girl? I told you braids aren't your look—they don't suit people like us."*

Surprise, Brocade, Shell thought. Braids do suit me. The small voice inside continued, What will Malcolm think? If he liked me before, will he like the way I look more now, or less?

"Where could they have gone?" Shell said only halfway to Bitsy, who had a turkey and cheese sandwich in one hand and a copy of *A Raisin in the Sun* in the other.

"Hmm?" Bitsy said, absentmindedly. "Soccer, probably. Sheesh. Shell, this is pretty intense. Who are you in the play?"

Shell said, "I'm going to play the mother, but just in one scene. Do you think I'll make a good brokenhearted mama?"

Bitsy laughed.

Shell decided to look in the garage to see which car was there. The garage was empty. "If they are at soccer, then why are both cars gone?"

Bitsy shrugged.

While Shell was looking around for a note, she noticed the answering machine message light blinking orange. When she played it, her mother's voice said slowly, "Shell, honey, we're at Grady Hospital. Honey, it's your dad. He's having some trouble with his heart. He should have been taken to Dekalb, but for some reason the ambulance driver brought him to Grady. Well, if you could come to the emergency room as soon as you —" and the tape ended, cutting off her last words.

"Oh, Shell!" Bitsy said, pale and shaken as she dropped her sandwich to her plate. Shell felt dizzy, like she'd been lying out in the sun and a huge cloud passed over head, leaving her cold in its shadow.

Bitsy drove Shell downtown to Grady Hospital. The emergency room at Grady felt crowded, impersonal, and chaotic to Shell, who'd never been to one before. First Shell and Bitsy just stood inside the sliding doors, clutching each other's arms and looking for Shell's parents. There were people, all sorts of people, sitting in the molded plastic chairs, standing by the walls, waiting in wheelchairs. It looked like a mess. Some people had obvious problems, with cloth pressed to cuts, while others looked glazed and generally ill. Shell wanted her mother to appear, hug Shell, and tell her that everything would be fine, that it was all a mistake.

After a minute or so of waiting, Shell approached an older woman behind a counter who appeared to be checking people in. The woman sensed Shell standing there and said "Name" without even looking up from her computer keyboard.

"Uh, it's not me. I mean, I'm not the patient. I'm looking for my father, William Wilkins?" Shell said, sounding unsure of her own voice.

The woman glanced at Shell, then pointed her toward another window. "You can check over there, hon. Next, please."

After waiting in a short line, Shell was told by another woman that her father was not in the emergency room anymore and that she wasn't quite sure where he was. "It looks like he's been admitted, but I don't know that he's in his room yet. Room 329. You can take the elevator and wait for him there."

Shell and Bitsy took the elevator to the third floor. Bitsy couldn't seem to stop talking once they were in the elevator alone together. "I swear, Shell, I can't believe this is happening. Did I ever tell you about the time that Beau broke his arm? He was like 14 or something, and he was climbing a tree, and . . . oh, wait, it wasn't that time, it was the time he wanted to be a stuntman in the movies, and he was trying to balance his bike on top of the garage roof like he saw that actor he liked so much do in that movie.

What was that guy's name? Not Stallone, not Arnold what's-his-name either, but one of those guys . . ."

Shell just looked at her, letting the words roll over her. They got off the elevator on the third floor and walked around, looking for Room 329. When they found it, Shell saw the door was open and the bed was empty. But when they walked in, Shell saw her mother sitting quietly on a chair by the bed.

"Shell," she said and stood up. Shell saw that her mother was wearing old shorts and a T-shirt, with her hair pulled back in a clip. She never went out like this, without makeup, in shorts. Shell felt a surge of protective love for her mom, who'd rushed out of the house this way.

"Mom? Is Dad okay?" They rushed to each other, and Shell's mom hugged her tight.

"He seems okay. The doctor thinks it's angina, but she wanted to run some tests to make sure he didn't have . . ." she hesitated just a moment, then went on, "anything more serious."

Shell, who was sensitive to what she wasn't being told these days, said, "What's angina, and what would be more serious? And where is he? And where's Ty? I thought they were both with you." Shell wanted to see them, to see every person in her family and to know that they were okay.

"They are running some more tests on your dad, but he should be brought up here soon. I'm not really sure what happened, except I was getting ready to take Ty to his soccer game, and your dad had gone to return his car to the dealer. Wilkie was upset about it, you know. He didn't want us to worry, but he hated to give that car back. He hardly slept last night, thinking about it. Oh, I'm sorry. I don't know why I'm crying," she said, interrupting herself to wipe her eyes with a soggy tissue. "Anyway, I had just dropped Ty at the game and was on my way to pick up your dad when I got a call from the dealer that your dad was having chest pains and they'd called for an ambulance. I called Shaun's mom and told her what had happened, and she said she'd take Ty to her house after the game. So I met the ambulance down in the emergency room. They did some blood tests right away, and then they took him for a chest X-ray and an ECG for starters."

"What's angina?" Bitsy asked.

"It's just what they call chest pain. It's actually a symptom of something else, not a condition in itself. The tests are to make sure he isn't having a heart attack," Shell's mother said, trying to smile calmly. But the way she squeezed Shell's hand gave her away.

Shell and Bitsy took this in. Then Bitsy said, "I'd better go call home to let them know where I am, okay?"

"You can use that phone, dear," Shell's mom said, pointing to a phone by the bed. While Bitsy called home, Shell's mom said, "And, Shell! Look at you! I didn't even get to tell you how beautiful you look."

Shell looked at her in surprise. What was she talking about? She glanced down at her T-shirt and jeans.

"Your hair, honey. You look so good in braids! Your dad is going to love them."

When Shell's dad was finally brought up to his room, he looked smaller somehow in the hospital bed, and his color was off. Bitsy only stayed for a few minutes, then headed home. "Call me if you need me for anything, okay?" she said.

Shell swore she would and thanked her for all of her help.

Shell thought of how angry she'd been with her father lately and how she'd wanted him to be the one to suffer over his job instead of her. "Dad, I . . . I'm so sorry," she said, heavy with shame. What if he died? He could have died, and then she would never have had a chance to tell him she loved him. "I didn't mean for you to . . ." Shell began, then started to cough and cry at the same time.

"What are you talking about, Shell? You didn't make this happen," he said. "I'm just an old worrier, that's my problem. Now come here and give me some sugar."

That's what he used to say to her when she was little. *Come give me some sugar!* Shell smiled and hugged her father gently, and he laughed, saying, "Now, Shell, do you think I'm as old as all that? I don't break that easy, girl." And she laughed, too, and felt better. Then he noticed her braids. "How long have I been in this place? Look at my girl!" he said to his wife, who smiled. Then he turned to Shell again, "Look at you! What a knockout you are growing up to be! A regular Miss America!"

Late that evening, the doctor made her rounds and stopped in to talk with Shell's parents about the tests. The doctor was a short, energetic Filipino woman with short, cropped hair, wire-rimmed glasses, and a slight accent. She said the tests confirmed that Shell's dad had angina from coronary artery disease and hadn't had a heart attack. Seeing their obvious relief, she said, "Yes, this is better that you did not have a heart attack. It is also good that your coronary artery damage is not severe. But there is not a cure for coronary artery disease, and your blood pressure is too high. And so I will recommend someone for you to see to monitor you. I do not think you need surgery. You will take nitroglycerine for the angina, and if you can reduce stress in your life, this will help too." She signed the forms to release Shell's father and shook his hand.

"Shouldn't they at least keep you overnight?" Shell's mom worried. Shell's dad shook his head. "It don't work like that, sugar. These insurance companies decide that now, and they say, 'He ain't dying, so he can sleep at home!' I'll sleep better in my own bed anyway."

When they finally picked Tybee up at his friend Shaun's house, Ty was waiting for them by the front window, looking forlorn and afraid, still in his shiny blue soccer uniform with his skinny knees sticking out of his soccer shorts. When he saw the minivan drive up, he ran out onto the dark driveway to meet them. "Dad, are you all right?" he asked, scrunching his eyes against the car's headlights.

His dad opened the passenger door to hug him and said, "I'm fine. I'm just sorry to give everybody such a scare."

Shell's mom said, "I'll go thank Shaun and his family. Then we can go on home."

Shell sat in the back with Ty. She was so glad to see him, she put her arm around him. "Dad," she said.

"Yes, Shell?"

"Are you really . . . I was so . . ." Shell couldn't finish the sentence. Her throat was too tight with tears.

"It's okay now, baby. I'm gonna be fine, and we still have each other. I have so much to be thankful for. I see that now," he said as he watched his wife appear in the lighted doorway, walk through the shadows of the yard, and then join them again in the warm van. "Let's go home," he said to her, stroking her hair lightly with his hand.

12

MAKING
MACARONI

JOURNAL,

Sunday night, and it seems like forever since last weekend when we first found out Dad was sick. We've had a week to get used to having one car, and it is a pain, but not as much as it will be when Dad gets a job again. He will get one, I know, and I hope he knows it. I hope he isn't giving up on himself. He's been quiet this week, like what happened with his heart scared him somewhere deep down. Or if it didn't scare him, maybe it made him think about things somewhat differently. He isn't looking for jobs in the paper, but when I asked, he said he's looking in himself to see what it is he really WANTS to do. Then he'll figure out who to talk to to make it happen. That life's too short to work just for money. "Okay, Dad," I said, "whatever you say." To think that I thought he just didn't care. One good thing that came out of his heart scare is that now I know he is worried about it all—getting a job, how Mom is doing, and my school. All that. And Mom is worried about him.

So Monday afternoon, after all the craziness of Dad being sick, I had my audition for drama. I'd been so worried about it, you know, but after what happened with Dad, the audition wasn't at all like I'd expected. I'd memorized some of Mama's lines from A Raisin in the Sun *by Lorraine Hansberry. In the scene, the mother is talking to her grown daughter, Beneatha, about Walter, Beneatha's brother, who has disappointed them both. As I sat in the classroom before the bell rang, I could hardly catch my breath. And I felt so tense, my jaw hurt. I just looked over at Malcolm and he smiled at me, patted his hair, and nodded approvingly. I was glad he was there, in a way, but it would have been a lot easier with just Evelyn. I tried to get into character and went on stage, pretending to be an older mother, disappointed in her son who'd lost the family's money, but trying to smooth things out between my grown children. When I got to Mama's speech about love, I really didn't think about my classmates who were lounging around on the floor, watching me. I didn't think about Evelyn who would be grading me and judging whether I was good enough to stay in her class. As I said the lines:*

Child, when do you think is the time to love somebody the most? When they done good and made things easy for everybody? Well then, you ain't through learning—because that ain't the time at all. It's when he's at his lowest and can't believe in hisself 'cause the world done whipped him so! When you starts measuring somebody, measure him right, child, measure him right.

I could feel the heat in my face, the truth of what I was saying like somebody else was saying it! I realized—to my horror!—that I was going to cry. My eyes were full, and I tried hard not to blink, knowing the tears would run out, but I couldn't stop them. There I was, on stage, crying for myself and for my dad. When I finished speaking my lines, I walked right off the stage and through the door to Evelyn's office. I just had to have a minute to clean myself up before I could look anyone in the eye again. I couldn't believe I'd cried. I was kicking myself for it, really mad, blowing my nose hard, and trying to settle down when Evelyn knocked on her own door, then came in.

"Shell," she said, "that was pure gold. Really fine. Welcome to my class. You obviously belong *here. I hope you will read through the whole play if you haven't already, because I am planning on making it our fall production, and I'd like you to try out for a part. Maybe Beneatha. See what you think, okay?"*

Can you believe that? I nodded but don't think I said a thing. I was so happy. So glad to belong somewhere and proud, too, that I'd earned her respect.

I'll write more later, maybe. Promised Mom I would help her get ready for her catered dinner tomorrow by making macaroni salad for her tonight while she is out with Audrey setting up.

Shell was down in the kitchen boiling big pots of water for the macaroni when the phone rang. It was Malcolm, calling her for the first time. She felt her heart leap in her chest as she fanned herself with the dish towel and tried to sound casual, like he called all the time.

"Oh, hi, what's going on?" she said.

"Not much," Mal said. "I was just wondering if I could come by for a while tonight. We could—uh—talk about drama, or something."

Well, that was pretty lame, Shell thought, but she said, "Um, you can come for a little while, but I have to make some macaroni salad for my mom. She's a caterer, and she asked me to help her out tonight. So, you know, if you don't mind just hanging out . . ."

"I don't mind," he said quickly. "In half an hour or so, okay?"

When Shell hung up she raced upstairs to change clothes, brush her teeth, and put on some lipstick. Then she checked to see what her dad and Ty were doing. They were in the family room. Her dad was reading the Sunday paper while Ty was lying on his stomach, surrounded by Legos. He was building something with both hands while he held the harmonica between his lips, breathing through it, in and out, like peaceful punctuation.

"Um, Dad? A friend of mine from school is going to stop by, okay?" Shell said.

"Okay," he said, turning a page of the sports section.

Mal showed up a little while later. He looked like he'd just showered, and he smelled spicy, like cologne. Shell invited him in, shyly. He followed her to the kitchen, where she made a big show of clearing off a space at the counter for him to sit and watch her as she cooked. It felt strange at first, but after talking for a little while, Shell felt perfectly natural, like they did this all the time.

"It feels like I've known you for years," Shell said as she chopped onion, celery, and olives for the dressing.

She went to drain the pasta when Mal said, "Let me help you." Mal took the pot holders from her, bowed, and carried the heavy pots of boiling water to the sink, where he drained the elbow macaroni into two colanders. Shell's eyes stung from the onions, and she blinked back tears. Mal grinned at her, then walked up and lifted her chin. "Now, now, you don't have to cry about it. I'll help you make macaroni anytime." Then he leaned closer still, closed his eyes, and kissed her. Shell kissed him back with her eyes open, a dish towel in one hand, and the other hand on his shirt. She was trying to concentrate on remembering just how it felt so she'd never forget, when she saw Ty coming through the doorway.

"Shell, look at my helicop—" Ty said, then stopped when he saw them. Mal heard him come in and turned to look. Ty stood for a second with his mouth hanging open, then he turned back around and walked back out.

"Who was that?" Mal asked with a smile. He was still standing close.

"My brother, Tybee. I, uh, I guess we'd better . . ." Shell gestured to the salad supplies.

"Oh, right," Mal said, half-seriously. He leaned past her for the parsley and sour cream. "What should we do with this?" he asked. Shell looked at the recipe. "Something about mixing it with the oil and vinegar . . ." When she looked up, he kissed her again.

Somehow, the salad got made and put in the refrigerator to cool. As Shell walked Malcolm to the door, she said, "Thank you for helping me with that recipe."

"Thanks for letting me come over," he said, stepping out into the porch light. "I hope we can make macaroni again sometime." He walked to his car, then turned around and walked back. "Shell?"

"Yes?" Shell said, amused by his seriousness all of a sudden.

"You know that Ocean Motion dance that's coming up? Would, uh, you like to go with me?"

"I'd really like that," Shell said. "'Night."

"Goodnight," Mal said with a grin. "See you tomorrow."

Shell closed the door gently, then leaned against it. He'd kissed her! And he'd asked her to a dance! She grinned and hugged herself tight to keep from screaming out loud. When she opened her eyes, her dad and Ty were standing there, staring at her.

"Everything okay?" her dad said. They looked so ordinary, from the ordinary world of newspapers and Legos. Shell wondered if she looked as different as she felt.

"Dad, everything is almost perfect."

13

TOASTED

WHAT, *you met somebody at Rainbow? What's he like? What kind of car does he drive? These French boys are très cute, mais not my type. Why, you ask? See Reason #258: Because the French like to wear the same outfits for three days straight. Love, Brocade*

Brocade,
Really, I don't think the car he drives would tell you anything—it's his parents' car. A four-door, dark red something. But he's . . . Shell couldn't think of how to describe Malcolm to Brocade. *He's in my drama class, and he's funny, but serious too. He asked me to a dance. I have no idea what to wear—the theme is ocean motion or potion or something. Shell*

Shell, it sounds like this guy is driving a Buick! You can't be serious. Really, guys our age just aren't worth the trouble. I'm thinking of just

waiting until I'm in college before I really date anybody. High school boys are so immature.
Brocade

Oh, please. What do you know? You don't know Malcolm, so leave him out of it, okay?
Shell replied, typing furiously.

Then she sent the message and shut down her computer. She'd just as soon ignore Brocade's emails for a few days, since she seemed to want to discourage Shell from seeing Malcolm. Was she jealous, or is it that she thinks he really isn't good enough? Shell wondered. Either way, she decided to stop filling Brocade in on what was happening for a while, and she was glad she hadn't told her about what happened the night Mal had helped her make macaroni.

At school Shell had a hard time concentrating on schoolwork. She kept thinking about going to the dance with Malcolm. She still couldn't believe he'd asked her. Shell realized this was something good that had come out of getting transferred to Rainbow—that when she made friends, they liked her for who she was, not because she was with Brocade. Shell knew that when she and Brocade used to be inseparable, she had felt safe with Brocade because people always looked at Brocade, not her. Brocade seemed to command attention and admiration from boys. Last year, Shell had felt accepted by everyone just by being with Brocade, but she had also felt invisible. Malcolm liked her for her. He didn't even know Brocade, and it didn't matter to him that Shell hadn't been to Europe. When she told him about Brocade's year abroad and how she'd wanted to go, he just said, "Why do you want to compare yourself to her, anyway? You can still travel later on if you want to. Life isn't over after high school, you know."

When Shell went to drama class, she saw Evelyn had posted notices about tryouts for *A Raisin in the Sun*. "There are ten parts, ya'll, so most everyone from this class who wants to be in the play will have that opportunity. I will allow other students to try out, though, so be sure to prepare well. Tryouts will be starting at the end of the week."

After class, Shell went to her locker, then looked around for Malcolm so she could walk to the bus with him. When she saw he wasn't in the classroom anymore, she started to walk to the front of the school by herself. As she rounded the corner, she stopped. Straight ahead, to the side of the front door, Shell saw Malcolm talking with Maya. They were standing close to each other, and Maya had her hand on Malcolm's arm. Like it belonged there. Like they were a couple. Malcolm wasn't pulling away; he was looking down into Maya's face. Shell was too far away to see his expression, but their body language told her all she needed to know. Instead of going on, Shell turned around and went to the back of the school where there were a few pay phones. She called home.

"Hello, Dad?"

"Shell? You okay, honey?" he said.

"I'm okay. I just missed my bus, though. Can you come get me?" Shell said. She felt a twinge of guilt, then thought it wasn't really a lie because by now she probably *had* missed the bus.

"No problem. Your mom just walked in. I'll be over in a few. Where should I meet you?"

"Behind the school," Shell said.

Later that evening, Shell called Bitsy and told her what she'd seen. "It was too good to be true," Shell said. "I should have known better."

Bitsy was unconvinced. "How do you know for sure? I mean, you didn't see him kiss her or anything, right?"

"I didn't need to. If I'd waited, though, I bet

I would have seen just that."

"Then why'd he ask you to the dance and not her?" Bitsy persisted.

"I guess he was just messing with me to make her jealous. I bet tomorrow he'll take back the invitation to the dance."

"When is the dance, Shell?"

"Friday night! What am I going to do?" Shell said. She felt empty inside. Not angry enough to confront Mal. She didn't even want to see him, in fact. She wanted to be back at Wainscott, invisible by Brocade's side.

"Well, crap. Do you have a dress yet?" Bitsy asked.

"Not a new one. I was going to call you to see if you could go shopping for one with me. Now I'm glad I waited. At least I didn't blow money on that—" Shell stopped. "Look, I'll call you tomorrow, okay?"

"Okay, but, Shell . . . at least ask him about it. Give him a chance to explain. You didn't really see anything conclusive . . ." Bitsy said, trailing off. "Isn't he worth that much?"

"Worth another chance to humiliate me? Oh, sure," Shell said sarcastically.

"If he does humiliate you, we'll get him. He's toast. History."

"Bitsy, I'm the one who was toasted."

14

OCEAN MOTION

FOR most of the next two days, Shell managed to avoid having a real conversation with Mal. On the bus, she sat by other people and avoided looking directly at him or Maya. In drama, she concentrated on the acting exercises and pretended he wasn't there. By Wednesday afternoon, Mal looked puzzled and caught up with her in the hall between classes.

"Hey, Shell. Wait up," Mal said as he touched her shoulder. Shell whirled around, furious. It was as though the extra time thinking about seeing him with Maya had made the incident larger and larger in her mind. The emptiness inside was gone now, replaced by anger.

"Why? Why should I wait?" she said,

"Because I want to talk with you," Mal said, looking hurt. His hand dropped to his side. "Look, I don't know what's wrong. I just wanted to see if you'd like to practice some lines from the play together. You know, it would be more fun that way."

"Well, Malcolm, let me think about it." She pretended to think. "No." Shell turned away and started to walk.

"Shell! What's wrong?" he said, keeping up with her.

"Mal, I know what you want to say to me. And it's okay. I don't mind. You can go to the dance with Maya. Let's just pretend you never asked me. Okay? Feel better? Now you don't have to bother with coming over to my house and acting like you care about this play . . ." Now that Shell was finally talking to him, she couldn't seem to stop talking. She looked over at him and saw something in his eyes that made her stop.

"Are you finished?" he said. Then he took her by the arm and said, "You got it all out yet? Because if so, then it's my turn."

The bell rang, and Shell realized the halls were empty. "I'm late for English!" she said in a panic.

"One tardy won't kill you," Mal said dryly. "Just hang on. Now what's this about Maya and the dance?"

Finally, Shell told him, "I saw you! I saw you talking with her on Monday, but it wasn't like you were just talking like to *anybody*. You looked . . . tight with each other, like there was something between you. So I figured—"

"So you assumed that I have a thing for Maya and that I really want to go to the dance with her?" Mal interrupted. "But you didn't just ask me about it right away; you waited two days until you were ready to blow up."

"Well, what was I going to say to you? You have every right to talk to Maya! I don't own you!"

"That's right," Mal said. "You don't. But I want you to know the truth about what you saw."

Shell felt a tremor in her stomach. "What is the truth?" she said.

"Maya and I liked each other last year. We sort of dated, if you can call it that. We were only sophomores; we couldn't go on real dates. But we broke up last spring. And that's it. It's long over. Okay?" He looked at her with serious eyes. "I don't want to go to the dance with anybody but you, Shell."

"Okay," Shell mumbled. "Look, I'm sorry . . ."

"You should be. Jumping to conclusions and I don't know what all . . . I think you owe me an apology in writing, maybe in a gold frame? Or how about some homemade cookies or . . ." Mal said, warming to the subject.

"Hey, do you two have hall passes?" Shell and Mal looked up to see the vice principal coming toward them.

"Uh, no, sir, we don't. We didn't realize the late bell rang already," Malcolm said.

The vice principal narrowed his eyes at them, but he couldn't seem to place them as troublemakers. He wrote late passes for them and sent them on their separate ways, saying, "Pay more attention to the bells from now on."

Shell was so relieved by her conversation with Mal that she could have hugged the principal. "Oh, thank you!" she said, taking the late slip and waving at Mal as she ran lightly up the stairs. The vice principal looked after her, surprised, then looked at Mal, who shrugged and grinned.

After school, Bitsy took Shell to a consignment store where she knew they had a great selection of dresses. "No problem," she said. "We will surely find the perfect dress." They found several dresses that looked great on Shell. She finally chose a beautiful raw silk sleeveless dress in a shade of coral.

"Are you sure it's not too dressy?" Shell asked Bitsy as she modeled it in front of the mirror.

"I think it's just right," Bitsy said admiringly.

"You could dress it up with jewelry or keep it simple. That color is great with your skin and hair. It would make me look anemic."

When they got back to Shell's house, the U.P.S. truck was just leaving. There was a big parcel leaning on the counter in the kitchen, and Shell's father was trying to figure out the best place to start cutting through the layers of tape and brown paper. Ty was pestering him.

"Who's it for? Is it something for me?" Ty demanded.

"No, not this time, Ty. Shell! I think your portrait arrived! Are you ready for the unveiling?" her dad said.

Shell and Bitsy helped hold the painting while Shell's dad worked on removing the paper.

"How come she gets a new painting, and I don't?" Ty asked. He was sitting on a chair, swinging his legs so his heels bumped into the kitchen cabinet. *Bump. Bump. Bump.*

"Cut that out, Tybee. Shell, I keep forgetting to remind you. Your mom has a big catering gig next Thursday. Her company was picked to cater the mayor's election-night party, so it's a big deal. Your mom wanted me to ask if you and a few of your friends might be interested in helping serve food. Audrey needs more people to help out. You'd get paid," he said.

"Sure, I'll do it," Shell said.

"Me too. Sounds like fun," Bitsy said. "As long as he wins, anyway. I'd hate to be at a party for the loser."

"Can I come too?" Ty begged.

"Sorry, kiddo. It'll go too late. We'll have to get a sitter for you," his dad said.

Ty thumped his heels hard one last time to make sure everyone knew how he felt about that, then he slouched out of the room mumbling, "It's not fair. She gets to do all the fun stuff!"

Shell's dad peeled away the last paper wrapping and came to a thick layer of bubble wrap. "I don't know if we'll ever get to see what this painting looks like," he joked. "The Wilkins family don't play around when it comes to wrapping packages. We are into serious tape. Ah, here we go." And he finally removed the last of the plastic.

Shell and Bitsy sat back on the kitchen floor and looked at the painting. "This Grandma Blue of yours is really good, isn't she?" Bitsy said. "That is so amazing. Do you realize how lucky you are? My grandmother knits plastic squares into tissue box holders."

Shell smiled. The painting showed Shell in Grandma Blue's backyard. Shell was shown from the waist up, turning to look back over her shoulder. There was a pink blooming vine by her hair, and the sun was shining down on her and the flowers like pure gold. Shell thought it was a pretty painting of a pretty girl, but she didn't feel that it could be her. She'd never really thought of herself as *pretty* before.

"Do I really look like that?" she said.

"Yes, it looks like you. Well, it looks like you a few months back, when she painted it. I think you've done some more growing up since the beginning of the summer," Shell's dad said. "Good thing we had her do the portrait when she did!"

Dear Journal,

I hope I never forget how much fun today was. First, we had tryouts for A Raisin in the Sun, *and I feel like it went really well. Malcolm and I played a brother and sister in a scene between Walter and Beneatha, and I used all that anger I'd had at him to play like I was furious with him. We won't know until Monday if we got parts or not. But I'm not even worried about it, because tonight was the dance! It was so much fun.*

First, I was really nervous about my dress and about dancing. But once Malcolm came to pick me up, I felt fine. He brought me roses, and Mom and Dad took pictures of us. I could tell he'd washed his parents' car because it was all shiny. The dance was so crowded that it was hard to actually dance at first, but after a while some people must have left, because we had more room. There were all these green and blue balloons, streamers, and posters of underwater sea creatures, and the D.J. kept playing that hip-hop "Ocean Motion" song. He must have played it five times! My feet were killing me from the heels, but I was having so much fun.

After we danced for a long time, we were hungry. I went to the bathroom before we left the dance to go to a restaurant. Maya and Kayrin came in while I was in the stall, so they didn't know I was there. They stood by the sinks and talked about Malcolm and me! I finally realized why I'd gotten confused that day when it looked like they were sweet on each other. Mal didn't have a crush on Maya—Maya still had a crush on him!

I felt so much better. I understood why Maya acted cold to me and why Mal had seemed gentle with her that day I saw them talking. I'm so glad it's all working out. I got more email from Brocade, and I could tell she just didn't get why I was upset with her. It was like she was sorry for me that I'm at Rainbow and she thinks I'm jealous of her. I emailed back and told her I'd see her when she came back at Christmas. It's funny—I was jealous, but I'm not jealous anymore, and I don't want to go back to Wainscott. I'm just worried about Dad now, that he gets a good job soon. We aren't talking much about his heart, but I know we are all thinking about it. If he gets a job he likes, I just know it will help.

15

RIBS

SHELL'S mother winked at her as she loaded food into the minivan. "Thanks for helping out, Shell," she said. "Now you're sure your friends know where the mayor's campaign center is?"

"Yep. Bitsy and Malcolm are going to meet us over there," Shell said. "Is there anything else I need to get from the house?"

The minivan was packed full of food and supplies. There didn't appear to be room for anything else, even if something *was* missing.

"No, I think we've got everything. Let's go on over."

The party grew louder and more cheerful as the evening went on and the mayor's lead grew steadily. Shell was grateful to Malcolm and Bitsy for helping out. It was a lot more fun with them around. Once Malcolm walked by with a tray piled high with mini quiches. He stopped by Shell, pretending she was one of the guests.

"Ma'am? May I interest you in a quiche?"

"No, thank you, sir. I'm holding out for the macaroni salad. I hear they have a world-famous recipe." She smiled at Malcolm.

"Ah, the lady has excellent taste." He bowed. "But seriously, you want one?"

"No, thanks, I'm really holding out for the barbecued ribs."

"Ribs? No kidding? Where?" Mal asked, perking up.

"In the back. Audrey just brought them over," Shell said as she and Bitsy filled rows of punch cups.

"Oh, please, save some for me!" Mal begged.

"Okay, but back to work or the deal's off!" Shell threatened, waving a ladle at him.

Hours later, Shell, Malcolm, Bitsy, Shell's parents, and Audrey all sat around in the back with their feet up.

"These ribs were so good that if that was all the payment for helping tonight, I'd still be satisfied," Malcolm said as he waved a bone from the pile in front of him.

"Is that so?" Audrey teased. "Sounds good to me." Everybody laughed at the look on Mal's face.

"Dad, tell me more about what happened with the mayor," Shell pleaded. Though they'd already talked hurriedly earlier in the evening, Shell's dad said, "I was just chatting with the mayor about European companies, and I explained how my old company had closed their offices here. He told me there was a gentleman at the party I should talk to, a lawyer in international business law who consults with European firms about the American market. When I spoke with the lawyer, he suggested we might consider a partnership in a consulting business for engineering firms like the one I'd worked for. He said he's a recent graduate, and since I have years of experience, we could work together to advise other engineering firms that are considering expansion."

"Well, that sounds good, right?" Shell said doubtfully. Her dad smiled and said, "Yes, it sounds like something I'd really like to do. There's no doubt we'd start small, just the two of us, but it's a solid idea, and the potential would be there to grow and eventually hire other people."

"Would this involve much travel?" Audrey said, teasing. "Because if you're planning on going off to Europe, you can't take your wife. After everybody tasted the good food tonight, they all wanted a card from me so they can call us for their parties. With all the good contacts we made tonight, we're gonna have plenty of work ahead."

"That's okay," Shell said quickly. "Because I happen to be available for travel from time to time, and I'd be more than happy to take her place."

"What about the flying part?" her mother said with mock outrage.

"I'll just picture myself on stage with my gold Oscar in hand for my role in the film remake of *A Raisin in the Sun*. I'll say, 'I'm grateful to my high school drama teacher, Evelyn, for her encouragement at such a tender age . . .' "

Her parents laughed. Her dad said, "If we don't clean up, we'll never get out of here. Who wants to wash these trays? Miss Best Actress?"

Mal said, "You forgot to thank me, your wonderful supporting actor, you ungrateful girl. Here." He threw a dish towel at her. "I'll wash if you dry."